Sick Of Singleness

A BIBLICAL GUIDE TO BREAKING FREE AND FINDING LOVE

HARMONY CLAIRE

WestBow
PRESS®
A DIVISION OF THOMAS NELSON
& ZONDERVAN

WestBow Press books may be ordered through booksellers or by contacting:

WestBow Press
A Division of Thomas Nelson & Zondervan
1663 Liberty Drive
Bloomington, IN 47403
www.westbowpress.com
844-714-3454

ISBN: 978-1-6642-8705-1 (sc)
ISBN: 978-1-6642-8706-8 (hc)
ISBN: 978-1-6642-8704-4 (e)

Library of Congress Control Number: 2022923307

Print information available on the last page.

WestBow Press rev. date: 1/10/2023

To Dr. Richard Ross and Dr. Johnny Derouen.
Thank you for training me how to wield
the Word of God effectively.
My greatest desire is that God would use me to influence
others for Him as He has used both of you.

Foreword

"God, when will it be my turn?" My heart cried as I watched from the sidelines as yet another bride and groom shared their first kiss as man and wife. Reading book after book containing what popular Christian culture said about being single, I began to find myself in a place of hopelessness. I began to ask myself,

1. Have we been thinking about this the right way?
2. What does God say about "dating," singleness, marriage, and sex?
3. Is it the same thing the church is saying?!

Sick of Singleness offers a fresh and honest perspective that poignantly addresses these issues with God's freeing grace. Harmony's experience as a student of God's Word and her personal experience as an "expert in the waiting game" makes her a voice of truth and empathy. Her conversational style compassionately encourages the reader to look at what God actually says about singleness and challenges us to act on those truths in faith. She also sheds light on the man-made roots and deceiving platitudes of what popular Christian culture says about dating and singleness. Packed with scripture, as well as humorous and relatable stories, this book is a renewed look into the Bible's teachings regarding matters of the heart.

If you are single, divorced, or even struggling in marriage and asking the questions "Do I have the 'gift' of singleness?" "Will I ever find my soulmate?" "Has God forgotten about me?" "Did I marry the wrong one?" and other such cries of the heart, then this is the book for you.

Erin Griffith Carter
Wife, mom, and Southwestern Baptist Theological Seminary graduate (Master of Arts in Christian Education, Minor in Women's Ministry)

Introduction

Have you ever been stuck at a red light—I mean, really stuck? At first, you don't notice. You jam to your radio for a few minutes, confident it will release you soon. Only it doesn't. You begin to notice that every other lane is moving forward in an orderly rotation except for yours. The traffic light is stuck on red, and so are you. At this point, you have two choices: You can remain at the red light indefinitely, or you can acknowledge that the system is broken and release yourself at the first safe opportunity. Stay stuck on red or move ahead, the choice is yours.

My love life was "stuck on red" for years. I had faithfully done whatever popular Christian culture touted as God's way to do romance. I read the books, made the promises, quoted the mantras, and joined the movements. To my surprise, instead of being promptly paraded down the aisle by white doves praising my faithfulness, I found myself securely stuck at the singleness red light for nearly a decade. I would still be there had it not been for one fateful day when I got sick of it.

Are you sick of singleness too? Are you frustrated by relational failure or the lack of a serious relationship? Do you desperately long for love, yet it always seems just out of reach? If so, this story is for you. My hope is that the frustrations and setbacks I share will comfort you with the knowledge that you are not alone. My prayer is that the breakthroughs and lessons I learned will free and empower you to make life-changing choices. Finally, my goal is that the triumph I experienced will give you hope that the love you desire can become a reality.

PART 1

SICK OF SINGLENESS

The Story Behind the Story

CHAPTER ONE

Shattered

His confession descended on my heart like an ominous cloud, so thick I could barely breathe.

"You did *what* last night?" I finally whispered, hoping against hope that I had misheard him.

The first man I had ever loved, my precious boyfriend, my Ricky, lifted his pain-stricken eyes to gaze mournfully into mine and reconfirmed my worst fear. I was so shattered I thought I was dreaming.

Wake up! I urged myself. *Open your eyes. This is just a nightmare.*

Our relationship had been going so well. Ricky loved me. At least that's what I thought. I still had a fresh bouquet and love note from him on my nightstand.

This can't be real! Ricky wouldn't do this to me. Please, God, let this be a dream. Please let me wake up!

I didn't wake up. This was my reality—my horrible, heartbreaking, faith-shaking reality. As Ricky continued to cry and beg for forgiveness, my mind began to replay our story, frantically searching for where I had gone wrong.

The Backstory

I had been praying and faithfully waiting for God to send me "the one" for years. I had read popular Christian culture's relationship books. However, despite following their advice religiously, I still had not found the love story I was searching for. Instead, I'd had a few ill-fated relationships, but nothing serious, and I was beginning to lose hope.

As I struggled with my singleness, I was asked yet again to serve in another wedding. The old saying "Always a bridesmaid, never a bride" haunted my thoughts as we prepared for the big day. The bride encouraged me not to lose hope. She just *knew* that God would also bring me my Mr. Right soon.

On the evening of the wedding, I walked down the ballroom stairs with the other bridesmaids and spotted a handsome groomsman gazing at me. He had sandy-blond hair, a perfectly trimmed beard, and the most sparking blue eyes I had ever seen.

"Who's that?" I whispered to the bride, intrigued.

"That's the best man, Ricky."

I couldn't resist stealing glances throughout the ceremony, and I was pretty sure I had caught him looking at me too. During the reception, Ricky lost a bet with the groom and had to perform a solo for the guests. At the end of his performance, he burst into self-conscious laughter and looked over at me.

Heaven help me, his eyes are even more mesmerizing when he smiles.

When the clock struck midnight, the wedding was complete, and it was time to say goodbye. Ricky approached, smiling broadly, and said how nice it was to have met me. Our eyes locked, sparks flew, and for a few brief moments, we were the only two people in the room.

The next week I got an excited call from my newly married friend. I barely had time to say hello before she burst out with her happy news.

"Ricky said you are the most beautiful woman he has ever seen, and he asked for your phone number! I told you that God had someone on the way. You guys are perfect for each other!"

And we were, or so it seemed. Ricky's love for God blew me away. He lived to tell the world about his Savior, Jesus Christ. I had never seen such devotion or love for the Lord. He made me love God more just by being with him. After spending a couple of months getting to know each other, he formally asked me to be his girlfriend. I spent some time praying and then wholeheartedly accepted.

We decided from the beginning that we wanted to honor God and each other in our relationship. We guarded each other's hearts—no kissing and only brief side hugs. We kept ourselves sexually pure. We even made sure we were never truly alone to avoid even the possibility of temptation. We attended church together and even shared the Gospel together. Our relationship was everything it should have been.

Ricky's voice cut into my wistful reminiscing and jerked me back to reality.

"I made a mistake," he said through tears. "I didn't realize what was happening until it was over. I am so sorry. Please forgive me."

I did forgive, but I knew I'd never be able to forget. As much as I still loved him, a sacred trust had been broken. There was no going back. All my hopes and dreams of what could have been had evaporated like one's breath on a cold day. It was over, and I was alone … again.

The Decision

I spent the first few days after the breakup in numb disbelief. No matter what I did, memories of Ricky were everywhere. Eventually, I retreated to my room and opened social media. There he was again! His face smiled beside mine in my profile picture. I quickly switched it to the previous shot, a solo of me at someone else's wedding.

How appropriate, I thought ruefully. *"All by Myself" should be the theme song of my life.*

I switched my relationship status back to its default setting—single.

Why do I always end up back here? Why can't I find the right one despite my best efforts? Why does love elude me at every turn?

"I am sick of singleness!" I yelled into the darkness in frustrated anguish.

It was the first time I admitted it to even myself. I had been taught that to be discontent with singleness was to be discontent with God. I had not allowed myself to acknowledge just how miserable I was until now. The admission was freeing but also disheartening. What on earth could I do about it? I had tried everything. Or had I?

I decided then and there to find a way out of this soul-crushing loneliness. Others had made it out. If they could, so could I. There was something keeping me in singleness, and I would leave no stone unturned until I discovered what it was.

CHAPTER TWO

Popular Christian Culture versus the Bible

First, I looked to the Christian community for a solution to my dilemma. I found books, sermons, and articles on navigating singleness, finding contentment in it, and even making the most of it, but none on how to get *out* of it.

I am sick of hearing about how to be a better single! I'm trying to escape singleness, not improve it!

I shared my frustrations with a newly married classmate, hoping she would give me some pointers. Instead, she proceeded to parrot the same message I was getting from popular Christian culture (PCC).

"My time of singleness was such a gift. I was able to focus on ministry and deepening my relationship with the Lord. God brought me my husband once I learned to be content with just Him. God already has the right one picked out for you. Keep waiting on the Lord. He will bring you your spouse when the time is right."

Her advice was nothing new. I had heard and accepted this

worldview without question my whole life, but now questions began swirling:

1. Why were Christian singles encouraged to embrace singleness and only choose marriage if it fell in their lap?
2. How was learning to be content in unwanted singleness the solution when God Himself created marriage and blessed it?
3. Why did the Christian community generally teach that it was more righteous to suffer well in singleness than to pursue marriage?
4. Where did this mindset start?

That day I began a quest to understand the origins of popular Christian culture's message to singles.

To understand what happened, we must take a stroll back in time. Grab your Giga Pet and Beanie Babies because we're going back to the nineties.

The Naughty Nineties

The nineties were a pivotal time in history, and as a blossoming teenager, I had a front-row seat. Technology was advancing rapidly and revolutionizing everything in its path. I remember the first time I saw a Nintendo 64. As one of the first 3D gaming systems, it was cutting edge. If you scored one of those, you were instantly the most popular kid on the block!

The nineties also brought us the Internet. I remember waiting expectantly for the dial-up connection. That sound was like a secret code unlocking the mysteries of the World Wide Web. The Web brought unprecedented access to information and connection. The sky was the limit. It was an exciting time to be alive.

Unfortunately, the golden age was not all rainbows and unicorns. The nineties saw a spike in illegal drug usage, particularly among the nation's youth.[1] D.A.R.E. T-shirts abounded, but so did the drugs. Many a naïve teenager unwittingly began a lifelong battle with a deadly addiction, including a cousin I idolized. The end of the decade also saw the horrors of the notorious Columbine massacre. And who could forget the infamous Y2K scare? In the words of Dickens, "It was the best of times, it was the worst of times, it was the age of wisdom, it was the age of foolishness."[2]

The nineties were not only an exciting but also a perilous time to come of age. Both the youth and adults were treading in an unchartered territory where both opportunities and dangers abounded. One such danger was the prevalence of promiscuity and unprotected sex, which resulted from the sexual revolution of the sixties and seventies. The licentiousness that had been countercultural just a few decades before was now readily accepted, even celebrated. In the words of John Wesley, "What one generation tolerates, the next generation embraces."

Embrace it we did. Take the massively popular show *Friends*, which debuted in 1994. It was about a group of six lovable friends in their twenties living up the single life in New York City. Their theme song was practically the background music of the decade. Sing it with me, "So no one told you life was gonna be this way … Your job's a joke, you're broke, your love life's DOA."

Speaking of love life, our beloved *Friends* saw quite a bit of action. According to the *Hollywood Reporter*, the show's six main characters had a total of eighty-five sexual partners among all of them. Such sexual freedom was no longer considered shocking. It was expected, natural even.

While *Friends* aimed at young twenty-somethings, some

---

[1] https://www.psychiatrictimes.com/view/resurgence-illicit-drug-use-90s-poses-challenge-physicians.

[2] *A Tale of Two Cities.*

movies like *Clueless* catered to those of us still in school. I remember the first time I saw it. The main character, fifteen-year-old Cher, lived for clothes and boys. She sneaked out to parties and hung out with older teens. One scene, in particular, stuck in my mind. She became interested in a classmate and confessed she was "clueless" about what to do. To get his attention, she began showing up to school in ever-increasingly sexy outfits. Her reasoning was, "Sometimes you have to show a little skin. This reminds boys of being naked, and then they think of sex."

As an awkward preteen, I thought Cher was the epitome of wisdom and sophistication. I decided to try some outfits like hers the next time my mom took me shopping. I was surprised at how grown-up I looked. I came out of the dressing room proudly, showing off my tight little bodycon/tube dress. Let me tell you that went over like a fart in church. My mom ordered me to change immediately. Then she bought me a dress that looked befitting of a five-year-old. She made me wear it to church the following Sunday with a giant matching bow in my hair. My mother's method was questionable, but her motives were pure. She knew something I didn't.

Sadly, both our *Friends* and *Clueless* were keeping a dirty little secret from us. They did not discuss the problems associated with the "free love" and sexy high school role models. By the mid-nineties, AIDS was the leading cause of death in America for adults between twenty-five and forty-four.[3] The nineties kicked off with the highest teen pregnancy rate ever recorded in the United States before or since.[4]

Partly in response to the hypersexualized pop culture and its pitfalls, Christians of various denominations started to call young people back to the standards of sexual and mental purity set out

---

[3] https://www.apa.org/pi/aids/youth/nineties-timeline

[4] https://www.cdc.gov/nchs/data/hestat/teenpreg1990-2002/teenpreg1990-2002.htm

in the Bible. In 1993, the Southern Baptist Sunday School Board launched an interdenominational sexual abstinence program called True Love Waits (TLW). It inspired and challenged teenagers and college students to commit to saving sex for marriage and solidify it with a pledge.

True Love Waits became wildly successful. At the 1994 rally, teenagers and college students signed 210,000 pledges displayed in the nation's capital.[5] Participants received a purity ring to wear on their left ring finger as a symbol of their commitment. Even young celebrities such as Miley Cyrus and the Jonas Brothers got on the bandwagon and sported purity rings for a while.

True Love Waits and other abstinence programs helped make abstinence cool again. This cultural shift led the younger generation back toward biblical morals and eventually became known as the Purity Movement. The change was refreshing, welcome, and I dare say very needed.

As the Purity Movement grew, zealous people committed to purity were eager to contribute. In 1997, *I Kissed Dating Goodbye* was published. The author was twenty-one-year-old Joshua Harris. Harris expressed his frustration with the shallowness he had experienced within the dating scene. He desired to influence his peers to choose a better, more godly way of finding a spouse. Harris's message was based on the premise that dating was the fast lane to superficial, ungodly relationships and sexual sin. To obtain true godliness, He urged his peers to adopt a "new approach" to romantic relationships. His method included avoiding dating altogether and delaying relationships until an unspecified "right time" to show "true love" to others and maintain the purity of the heart.

I Kissed Dating Goodbye was hugely successful and revolutionized the Christian dating scene. It sold approximately

---

[5] https://www.encyclopedia.com/religion/legal-and-political-magazines/true-love-waits

1.2 million copies and became *the* textbook for Christian romance. Other honorable mentions from that era are *Quest for Love* by Elisabeth Elliot (1996), *Romance God's Way* by Eric and Leslie Ludy (1997), and *When God Writes Your Love Story* also by the Ludys (1999).

Around the time these books were popular, the Christian narrative concerning romance, love, and relationships began to change. It was no longer enough to "just" save sex for marriage. Now a plethora of additional standards, expectations, and practices were added to the mix to truly please God. Young people eager to prove their righteousness competed to see who could be more "pure" by exercising the most restraint in matters of the heart.

"You're saving sex for marriage? Well, I'm not even going to kiss until my wedding day."

"You're saving yourself physically? Well, I'm guarding my heart so that I don't give away any of myself emotionally to anyone but my spouse."

"You're pursuing romantic relationships? I'm waiting on God to send me the right one."

"You're interested in romantic relationships? I'm content just focusing on my relationship with God."

On and on it went until a new philosophy was born, known as purity culture.

Purity Culture

Here is the message in a nutshell: God has great plans for your love life and wants to give you His best. To receive God's best, you need to surrender control of your love life to God. God has already chosen the "right one" for you. He will lead you to them in His perfect timing. Your job is to pray, wait on the Lord, and be content in singleness until He does. To receive God's best, you must keep yourself pure in mind and body. Guard your heart when in a relationship so that you can be sure to give all your love to only your future spouse. Adhering to these standards will enable you to remain pure and enjoy romance God's way. God will reward you for your faithfulness by writing you a beautiful love story. However, deviating from these standards risks relational failure, heartbreak, and missing out on God's best.

The message of purity culture caught on life wildfire. We heard it preached from the pulpits, saw it in Christian teen magazines, and were gifted the latest books concerning it. Well-intentioned leaders in the church taught the message as if it were the Gospel, and many singles obeyed it. Some received their promised God-written love story, while others, like myself, found themselves still stuck in singleness decades later.

The years had tamed the message, but I recognized the same mindset within the advice I was receiving from the Christian community regarding my "sick of singleness" problem.

"Wait on the Lord."

"He will bring you the right one."

"Trust God for His best."

But what if this wasn't God's best? What if all this wasn't of God at all?

CHAPTER THREE

Merely Human Rules

As the eldest of my three siblings, one of my primary roles growing up was to act as my mother's mouthpiece. If Mom wanted something done or a message delivered, she often sent me in her name. The power to walk into a room and be obeyed because the wrath of Mom backed my words was quite exhilarating. It didn't take me long to realize that I could embellish Mom's message and still have it obeyed as if the whole thing came from her.

Religious leaders are to the church what I was to my siblings. They have the high calling of speaking on God's behalf. With that calling comes the responsibility to teach doctrines rooted in scripture, not just their own opinions. Unfortunately, just like a bossy elder sibling, sometimes leaders feel "led" to add a little of their own thoughts to "help God out." Though their hearts may be in the right place, a dangerous line is crossed whenever people start presenting their views and opinions as God's.

As I continued my quest for answers, I recalled a recurring theme in both the nineties purity culture doctrines and the more recent teachings I was receiving from popular Christian culture regarding singleness. Their message was often described with phrases like "God's best," "God's way," and "God's definition of love."

I reasoned that such bold claims of God's direct endorsement would undoubtedly be backed by scripture, yet I couldn't recall reading any of these teachings in the Bible.

I must be missing something.

I pulled some popular Christian books on singleness off my bookshelf and flipped through them, looking for direct scriptural support for their doctrines. To my great surprise, it wasn't there.

It must be here! I thought. *I've been taught these things like they were Gospel my whole life!*

My love life had been like a Jenga game. I constantly weighed every decision and action against popular Christian culture's endless rules, standards, boundaries, promises, and warnings. I had never even thought to challenge any of the doctrines I was continually dancing around until now.

Is all this really "God's" way? Or is it just a bunch of people's opinions?

The very thought seemed to cause the PCC's Jenga tower to wobble, then it stopped as if daring me to challenge its authority. Undaunted, I pressed on.

If these teachings are of God, they will stand up to whatever scrutiny I bring against them. If they aren't, then I want no part of it anymore.

My first step was to start searching the scriptures for myself. No more taking anyone's word for it. What did God really say about love, romance, finding a spouse, and singleness? I had a lot of ground to cover, so I first started with what I thought would be the most extensive topic—premarital relationships.

What was God's rule book for premarital relationships?

To my great surprise, it was not extensive at all. In fact, searching the Bible cover to cover only yielded two direct commands within scripture regarding premarital relationships.

Rule	Scriptural Support
1. Don't have sex outside of marriage.	Heb.13:4 1 Thess. 4:3–5 1 Cor. 6:18–20
2. Don't marry a nonbeliever if you are a believer.	2 Cor. 6:14[6] 1 Kings 11:1–6

If these two rules are enough for God, why does popular Christian culture have so many dos and don'ts when it comes to finding a spouse?

Torah versus Talmud

Man-made extra-scriptural standards have been around for millennia. In biblical times, they were referred to as the Talmud. God had given the Jews the law, which they called the Torah. Within the Torah, God had included various rules and regulations concerning cleanliness, purity, worship guidelines, and human relationships, to name a few. Over time, religious leaders began to add to it. Over the years, many traditions further expounding on what God initially said came into everyday practice. This collection of extra-biblical standards became officially known as the Talmud. The Talmud traditions were so strictly adhered to that they became doctrines that were revered as if they were God's Word.

Jesus had some choice words for these man-made doctrines. Enjoy this story with me.

> The Pharisees and some of the teachers of the law
> who had come from Jerusalem gathered around

[6] The context of 2 Corinthians 6:14–15 is not directly speaking about marriage. However, the principle contained in this passage is applicable to marriage.

Jesus and saw some of His disciples eating food with hands that were defiled—that is, unwashed (The Pharisees and all the Jews do not eat unless they give their hands a ceremonial washing, holding to the tradition of the elders. When they come from the marketplace, they do not eat unless they wash. And they observe many other traditions, such as the washing of cups, pitchers, and kettles; *Mark 7:1–4 NIV*).

Within the Torah, God had provided specific cleanliness guidelines for social and health purposes. However, the Talmud's extra standards demanded more and even stated that those who did not observe the expanded standards would be defiled, not just in body but also in soul. Therefore, naturally, the keepers of the Talmud were aghast that Jesus's followers were not adhering to the culture's extra-scriptural rules, so they decided to confront Him.

So the Pharisees and teachers of the law asked Jesus, "Why don't your disciples live according to the tradition of the elders instead of eating their food with defiled hands? (*Mark 7:5 NIV*)

The religious leaders had dared to speak unbidden on God's behalf, but Jesus did not have it.

He (Jesus) replied, "Isaiah was right when he prophesied about you hypocrites; as it is written: These people honor me with their lips, but their hearts are far from me. They worship me in vain; their teachings are *merely human rules*." You have let go of the commands of God and are holding on to human traditions (*Mark 7:6–8 NIV*).

Jesus took a pin to the religious leaders' power-trip bubble and popped it. Only God's commands are binding. Everything else can be neatly classified as *merely* human rules. This truth liberated me. I no longer had to juggle popular Christian culture's endless rules in a desperate attempt to be deemed godly enough to be awarded a spouse.

Although I was free from the "rules," I wanted to be cautious not to throw out the baby with the bathwater. Just because these teachings didn't come straight out of the Bible didn't necessarily make them bad. Human advice can still be helpful, depending on which human it's coming from. I began wondering, *Did the message of purity culture truly originate in the nineties, or was there more to the story?*

Sadly, there was more—much, much more.

The Rest of the Story

In the 1970s, a man named Bill Gothard began a ministry that eventually became known as the Institute of Basic Life Principles (IBLP). It was initially aimed at youth, and its stated purpose was to help people develop good character by applying biblical life principles. Gothard's principles covered almost every area of life, including romantic relationships. His views were ultra-conservative. For example, parental permission was required for marriage and courtship, contraception of any kind was prohibited, and divorce for any reason was denied. His severe teachings were not widely accepted and primarily affected only those within his own movement until his message influenced Elisabeth Elliot.

Elliot was a famous, well-respected missionary most known for her book *Through the Gates of Splendor*, published in 1957. It recounts the inspiring story of her, her husband Jim, and their companions' selfless ministry to the Huaorani tribe in Ecuador. *Through the Gates of Splendor* launched Elliot into the public eye and began her career as a Christian speaker and author. Her writing and ministry were primarily focused on the importance of submitting one's will to God. Elliot was a contemporary of Gothard's and was invited to speak at IBLP seminars. The IBLP often held her up as an example of biblical womanhood and submission.

In 1984, Elisabeth Elliot wrote a book titled *Passion and Purity: How to Bring Your Love Life under God's Control.* As you can see from the title, she took her core message of submission into the realm of romantic relationships. Her book emphasizes the importance of surrendering your love life to God's timing and waiting for His direction. Elliot uses her own love story with her first husband, Jim, as the model for this approach.

Not surprisingly, Elliot's views on love and romance in *Passion and Purity* are similar to Gothard's teachings on the subject from the seventies. In the hands of a hyperconservative leader like Gothard, such views remained relegated to his own movement. However, when the same ideas were championed by a Christian superstar such as Elliot, they became more palatable. So palatable, in fact, that Joshua Harris's mother gifted him with his very own copy of *Passion and Purity*.

In his book *I Kissed Dating Goodbye*, Harris shares that although he was initially put off by the title of Elliot's book, upon reading it, the book had a profound impact on his life. He even credits Elliot's love story and calls to purity as what inspired him to rethink his own attitude and approach toward romance. Harris's "new approach" wasn't new at all. In fact, the IBLP teachings regarding courtship bear a striking similarity to the core teachings in *I Kissed Dating Goodbye*.[7]

Elliot made Gothard's message palatable, and Harris made it popular, so popular that it transformed popular Christian culture's romance narrative.

This would all be a superfluous history lesson were it not for the

---

[7] https://iblp.org/questions/how-does-courtship-work

fact that Bill Gothard stepped down as the leader of the IBLP in 2014 after numerous allegations of sexual abuse were brought against him by former teen interns of his ministry. Subsequently, the IBLP had a lawsuit brought against them by several female plaintiffs in 2015 for failing to address the alleged abuse. Gothard himself had a sexual harassment/abuse lawsuit brought against him in 2016.[8]

The lawsuits sparked public interest in the inner workings of the IBLP. "The Cult Next Door," a 2016 *Chicago Magazine* article, shares testimonies from alleged female victims who recall being asked to late-night one-on-one meetings where *accidental* touches were a little too frequent and *friendly* affection was just a little too intimate. The women confided that they did not initially press charges because Gothard was so revered by their community, it was as if he was God.[9]

Although the lawsuits were withdrawn in 2018, partly because of the statute of limitations, the investigation into the IBLP continues. As I write this book, Amazon has a docuseries in the making investigating the IBLP organization, teachings, and prominent followers, including the Duggar family.[10]

My discoveries regarding the origins of purity culture's doctrines surprised and distressed me. Sadly, the story was far from over. The message that was initially so well received had unintended consequences that resulted in a shocking fallout.

---

[8] https://www.nbcnews.com/news/us-news/ministry-nourished-duggar-familys-faith-falls-grace-rcna14024

[9] https://www.chicagomag.com/Chicago-Magazine/July-2016/Institute-in-Basic-Life-Principles-Hinsdale/

[10] https://variety.com/2021/tv/news/duggars-documentary-investigative-series-amazon-lularich-1235142307/

The Fallout

The initial success of *I Kissed Dating Goodbye* launched Harris into a long and prosperous career in ministry that included authoring many popular books, hosting conferences, and pastoring a megachurch. All seemed well until Harris resigned from his pastorship and stated that he felt he had gotten it all backward. He had begun leading in ministry before receiving any formal theological training. Off to seminary, he went. While there, he encountered peers who claimed that *I Kissed Dating Goodbye* had negatively impacted their view of themselves, their romantic relationships, and even their faith. Harris was also called out on social media by wounded readers who shared testimonies such as the following;

"@HarrisJosh honestly, your book was used against me like a weapon. But now, I just feel compassion for the kid you were when you wrote it."[11]

"@HarrisJosh Add me to ur IKDG victims. 37, never married, now infertile. Set bar too high cause of ur book. Many regrets!"[12]

"I'm a 30-year-old man who has never had a girlfriend, never been on an actual date, never asked anyone out, and never kissed anyone. That's on me. Nevertheless, I suspect that without IKDG and the movement surrounding it, that wouldn't be the case."[13]

In response to the "growing number of voices of people who have been hurt,"[14] Harris produced the documentary *I Survived I Kissed Dating Goodbye* to reevaluate the book's message. He expressed regret over the "shortcomings of my book and the culture it fostered." The documentary came as a surprise to many and received mixed reviews. Some praised Harris for his honesty,

---

[11] https://www.christianpost.com/news/abstinence-author-pastor-joshua-harris-apologizes-for-telling-christians-not-to-date-in-i-kissed-dating-goodbye.html

[12] ibid

[13] ibid

[14] ibid

while others expressed disappointment with his new conclusions. Then came the final fallout.

In 2019 Harris shocked the Christian world by announcing that he was separating from his wife and his faith. Harris stated, "I have undergone a massive shift in regard to my faith in Jesus. The popular phrase for this is "deconstruction," the biblical phrase is "falling away." By all the measurements that I have for defining a Christian, I am not a Christian."

The fallout was indeed great, and it cost so many, so much, which begs the question: How did this happen?

How it Happened

How did the purity movement's call to chastity mushroom into a message that thwarted the very love it promised to deliver? Extrabiblical doctrines distorted popular Christian culture's romance narrative because believers failed to do their due diligence. We chose to rely on human leaders to spoon-feed us doctrines instead of doing the hard work of digging into the scriptures ourselves. We failed to measure their teachings against God's actual Word. We forgot that even the most well-intentioned leaders are not without error or above deception.

We must be very cautious of the human messages we allow to influence us. Just because someone we like or respect stamps God's name on something doesn't mean their message originated with God. We must double-check the teachings of even those we trust against scripture.

Once I realized that I had the permission and *responsibility* to challenge the teachings presented to me, I decided to launch a full-blown investigation into popular Christian culture's message to singles. I discovered that the added human rules were just the tip of the iceberg. A faulty theology at the core of the message had caused heart issues that needed to be dealt with.

CHAPTER FOUR

Gumball Theology

Do you know those gumball machines often placed at the entrance to grocery stores? I was obsessed with getting one of those gumballs when I was a kid. I always looked at them longingly when I went in with my mom. She did not believe in wasting money on them. One day I went in with Dad, and he gave me a quarter! I rushed to the machine, put in my quarter, and turned the knob with great anticipation. Then the unthinkable happened—the knob jammed; both my quarter and gumball were held hostage. My dad didn't have any more quarters, so he offered to get me some stick gum at the checkout line. I couldn't believe it. My one chance to get a gumball and now it was gone. I had been betrayed by a double-crossing gumball machine

Gumball theology, as it is popularly called, assumes that God's actions, blessings, and gifts are a direct result of people's behavior, good works, or attitude toward Him. Here are some popular examples:

- God will heal you if you have faith.
- God will enrich you if you tithe.
- God will answer your prayers if you believe.

21

Regardless of the particulars, gumball theology typically follows a formula similar to the following: "God will (fill in the blank) if you (fill in the blank)."

According to this mindset, all that is required to receive your desires from God is to insert your quarter of obedience, trust, submission, etc., and God will release the gumball of marital happiness, financial stability, business success, or whatever it is you are bargaining for.

In matters of love, popular Christian culture teaches that purity is the currency needed to buy relational prosperity from God. I first heard about this deal at summer camp in my freshman year of high school. The speaker was giving the ever-popular abstinence message, but this time, instead of scaring us with the possibility of sexual disease or teen pregnancy, he employed a different means of motivation.

"Teenager, if you will trust God and keep yourself pure now, then He will bless you with the truly special wedding night and awesome love life that is possible when we obey Him."

It is quite a bargain when you think about it. A few years of waiting, obeying, and forgoing fun in exchange for a lifetime of relational bliss—sign me up, Lord!

Many of my peers and I did sign up. We committed to saving ourselves for marriage and then eagerly waited for God to make our dreams come true. Some received their gumball of marital happiness quickly, while others were left disillusioned in prolonged singleness. We put in a quarter of purity but received no gumball in its place. Where did we go wrong?

The SOS Club

The SOS Club, a little band of singles who were sick of it, congregated in a coffee shop and waited for their orders. They didn't mind waiting; by this time, they were used to it. The conversation soon turned to the topic of romance or, rather, the lack thereof. Misery loves company, so each of them took turns mourning into their mochas as they shared their stories.

"I did everything right," Anne lamented.

She shared that she had faithfully waited for years to receive the promise of marital happiness. When her boyfriend had proposed the previous year, Anne was elated. God had finally sent her "the one"! Sadly, the wedding was abruptly called off because of her discovering that her fiancé was not who she thought he was.

Anne felt lied to by God. How could He let this happen? Where was the reward of relational and marital prosperity in exchange for her faithfulness?

"I saved myself for years, and God rewarded me with shattered dreams and a broken heart while others slept around and got loving husbands anyway. I guess I should have just done like them," Anne concluded in dejection.

Gumball theology set Anne up for failure because it made an unauthorized promise on God's behalf. God does not guarantee prosperity in exchange for obedience. The Bible warns believers that obeying God will often result in hardship. When Jesus was choosing His disciples, He was frank about the life He was calling them to:

> "If anyone wants to follow after me, let him deny himself, take up his cross, and follow me" (*Matthew 16:24*).

To be a genuine disciple, the cost will be self-denial, trials, and often relational hardship. Jesus went so far as to warn that lining up with Him could even cost one their life.

> Brother will betray brother to death, and a father his child. Children will even rise up against their parents and have them put to death. You will

be hated by everyone because of My name. But the one who endures to the end will be saved (*Matthew 10:21–22*).

God does not promise one thing and then deliver another. If you have been double-crossed by gumball theology, understand that your anger is valid, but it should not be directed at God. Doing everything "right" does not guarantee that you will experience relational success and avoid all pitfalls. Once you accept that, you will free yourself from disillusionment and doubts when your righteousness does not excuse you from the trials of life.

Contrary to gumball theology, our relationship with God is not transactional. God does not owe us when we are obedient. Jesus Christ is the only Person who lived His life perfectly, and He was falsely accused and murdered for someone else's crimes. If the Son of God suffered despite living right, who are we to demand a reward from God for good behavior?

SOS Round 2

After Anne finished venting, Andy chimed in.

"What are you doing here, Mitch?" he asked in an overly chipper voice. "Didn't you have a date tonight?"

Mitch rolled his eyes.

"I did, but it felt more like an interview than a date. She spent the majority of the meal asking me questions about my past relationships. When I asked her why she was so interested, she said that she wanted to know if I had kept myself 'pure' like she had. I joked that if she was looking for a sinless man, then she should just keep on 'dating Jesus.'"

"Wow! Burn, dude!" Andy chuckled. "That's really frustrating, man," Andy went on. "It seems like any degree of 'stumbling' in the relationship department is grounds to disqualify someone or, at the very least, put them at the bottom of the list. Honestly, if one mistake is enough to permanently wreck one's future love life, what's the point of even trying?"

If the mood was somber before, it was downright dark after that. The friends tried to encourage one another not to give up. Surely, there was still hope for them to find love. After their mochas were gone and goodbyes said, they went home to their empty houses and tried to sleep, but the shared sentiments continued to swirl around in their minds.

> *Pure = sinless relationships*
> *Stumbling = wrecked love life*
> *No point trying*

They began to wonder, *With standards like these, how did anyone ever succeed in love? Who could ever measure up?*

Can you identify with any of the sentiments expressed by the members of the SOS Club? I sure did. Have you ever wondered where these sentiments come from?

For me, it all started with a pair of socks.

1 Sock, 2 Sock, Red Sock, Blue Sock

I'll never forget the object lesson used on that hot summer night at summer camp. The youth leader held up a piece of clear scotch tape, representing someone in their "pure" state. Then he began to stick the tape to different colored socks, each symbolizing a different sexual partner. Finally, he tried to attach the sullied, barely functional piece of tape to a fresh white sock. The tape could no longer stick well and ended up tarnishing the white sock.

"This is what will happen to you if you don't keep yourself pure until marriage," the youth pastor said solemnly. "Not only will you diminish your own value, but your sexual sin will also end up harming the person you will one day marry."

The silence was thick as we soberly looked at the dirty, useless tape. Those who had managed to keep themselves pure breathed a sigh of relief that their future marriages still had a chance. In contrast, those who hadn't were left with the impression they had forever compromised God's plan for their life.

PCC teaches that Christians who have kept themselves "pure" from sexual sin will forfeit the benefits they have worked so hard to obtain if they marry someone who is "impure." The result is a type of Christian elite that must keep themselves separate from their *more* sinful brothers and sisters. Jesus called out this "better than others" attitude among the religious elite of his day.

To some who were confident of their own righteousness and looked down on everyone else, Jesus told this parable:

> Two men went up to the temple to pray, one a Pharisee and the other a tax collector. The Pharisee stood by himself and prayed, "God, I thank you that I am not like other people—robbers, evildoers, adulterers—or even like this tax collector. I fast twice a week and give a tenth of all I get." But the tax collector stood at a distance. He would not even look up to heaven but beat his breast and said, "God, have mercy on me, a sinner." I tell you that this man, rather than the other, went home justified before God. For all those who exalt themselves will be humbled, and those who humble themselves will be exalted (*Luke 18:9–14 NIV*).

Mic drop! God is impressed with humility, not self-righteousness. Treating intact virginity as a prize that qualifies some while disqualifying others is not only unbiblical, but it is also sinful.

One and Done

Perhaps the most damaging message in purity culture is the portrayal of sexual sin as the one you can never quite come back from. *I Kissed Dating Goodbye* begins with a memorable illustration that rivals even the dirty sock bit for the most poignant.

A bride on her wedding day notices a trail of ex-girlfriends standing behind her groom. When she asks what's going on, he apologizes that he has given away pieces of himself to all these other girls, but she can have what's left.

These illustrations were meant as motivation to avoid the shame and brokenness of sin. However, an unintended consequence of these illustrations was the message that everyone who stumbled was somehow forever tainted. Jesus would forgive you, *but* there would always be part of you that you could never get back, just like that lost quarter.

Those illustrations are partly right. Sexual sin, like all sin, causes harm, pain and destruction...but God.

But God

But God is one of the most beautiful phrases in all of the Bible. In fact, gumball theology would be true were it not for this phrase. Read this verse with me:

> And you were dead in the trespasses and sins in which you once walked ... and were by nature children of wrath, like the rest of mankind. *But God*, being rich in mercy, because of the great love with which he loved us, even when we were dead in our trespasses, made us alive together with Christ—by grace you have been saved (*Ephesians 2:1–5 ESV*).

This is the power of the Gospel. It does not stop at salvation from hell; it also extends into life. Look at what Jesus said regarding His work on our behalf:

> The thief comes only to steal and kill and destroy;
> I have come that they may have life, and have it to
> the full (*John 10:10 NLT*).

The doctrines that demand perfection in your dating history to achieve marital happiness place their trust in a person's ability to be righteous and not in Jesus. They are partly right. People cannot restore their purity once lost ... but God can.

Remember my gumball story? I only told you half of it. I was so distraught over being swindled that my dad started going after that gumball machine. He was very mechanically inclined and just knew how things worked. To this day, I don't know how he did it, but he managed to not only get my quarter back but a gumball as well. What I couldn't do, my dad took care of for me. It was as if the loss of my quarter had never happened.

That is what God can do for us. If we all could live a sinless life, then gumball theology would have merit, but we can't. Jesus came to make an abundant life possible despite sin. Of course, there are consequences, but we serve a God specializing in giving beauty for ashes. He says that He can remove our sins as far as the east is from the west and cast them into the sea of God's forgetfulness. All we have to do is confess and repent.

What about you? Could you use the restorative power of the Gospel in your own life? Has this chapter revealed any heart issues that you need to repent of? Do you need a "But God"?

By the power of Christ, your past sins need not haunt your future. By the blood of Christ, your inevitable failures, whether sexual or otherwise, will not destroy your potential for future happiness in marriage.

Gumball theology portrays a worldview where the work of

Christ has no place. I don't want to live in that world. If my happiness is dependent on my ability to get it "right" every time, my sinful self is doomed. *But God* would not have it that way.

Once I truly grasped the wonder of the gift of forgiveness I had been offered, my relationship with God became marked by gratitude instead of expectations. With my heart in the right place, I was ready to move on to discovering the specific doctrines that were keeping me stuck in singleness. The first culprit was the gift that just wouldn't stop giving.

PART 2

SPIRITUAL ROADBLOCKS

Doctrines That Prolong Singleness

CHAPTER FIVE

The Gift

Winter may be a glistening wonderland for some, but in the Southern United States, winter is where dreams go to die. Unfortunately, I was so preoccupied with Ricky and I's breakup that the dreaded season sneaked up on me. The first freeze had struck during the night, turning the typically lush seminary gardens into a barren wasteland. The grass that had been green the night before was now brown and crunchy. The flowers that had proudly displayed vibrant blooms barely twelve hours ago now bowed low, limp, and soggy.

Ironically, the suddenly devastated landscape was comforting. It was as if the earth itself was mourning my broken heart with me. A short while ago, Ricky and I had strolled this path hand in hand. Now I would be walking it alone once again. My depressing musings were interrupted by the sound of joyful laughter. I looked up and spotted a couple of starry-eyed fellow students strolling, intertwined in each other's arms. They had just gotten married at the end of the fall semester.

"Ring by spring," wasn't that the unofficial seminary slogan?
They look so cute together. If only …

33

It seemed like God had come through for everyone except me. I rounded the corner and faced the imposing, colonial-style chapel looming authoritatively over me. It chided my longing and reminded me of my reason for being there. I had come to seminary to study and prepare for ministry, not get my MRS degree.

Still, I wondered, *Why did God choose marriage for so many others but not for me? I must have the dreaded "gift of singleness."*

If you have been a Christian single for any length of time, you have probably heard of this doctrine. It is one of the primary ways popular Christian culture seeks to console and encourage singles struggling with their supposed "calling." The gist of the doctrine is that God gives some a gift/calling to remain unmarried for either a season or the whole of their life. The teaching is based on the belief that individuals don't get to *choose* their gifts. God wisely chooses for them, and since His gifts are perfect, the gift of singleness must be accepted regardless of the individual's desires or preferences otherwise.

This doctrine influences many singles to avoid pursuing or even thinking about dating because they are afraid to appear ungrateful or resistant to what God has chosen for them. Hence, the "gift of singleness" becomes a self-fulfilling prophecy.

Mitch and Misty

Mitch was excited as he walked into the singles service that night. A charming girl named Misty had recently started coming to his church. She had been stealing glances at him, so he decided to invite her to coffee after the singles service that week. She showed up that Wednesday looking especially pretty, and her face lit up when she spotted him. They took a seat beside each other as the service started.

Mitch had difficulty concentrating on the worship with such a gorgeous girl beside him. Still, he managed to regain focus for at least one song. While the announcements were being made, he started thinking about how he should suggest the coffee date. Should he ask just her or try to make it more of a double-date? He pulled out his phone in search of a wingman, only to be abruptly interrupted.

"Hey, everybody!" an unfamiliar voice boomed.

Mitch looked up, startled, then hurriedly put his phone away. The hip guest speaker was making his ascent. He continued his greeting as he finished his energetic sprint to the podium.

"We will be covering a topic that applies *especially* to all of you tonight—the gift of singleness!"

The crowd laughed and groaned as Mr. Hip continued, "I know, I know, many of you are looking forward to marriage, and I see some of you are already quite cozy with the person next to you ..."

Mitch instinctively moved away from Misty. Was it that obvious?

"Romantic relationships are great," Mr. Hip admonished, "but they can distract you from God's *greater* purpose for your life. I'll bet many of you have already found yourselves distracted even during worship tonight because you were thinking about someone."

Mitch felt his cheeks get hot. He had tried to focus on the worship, but Misty just smelled so good. He chided himself for not sitting elsewhere and approaching her afterward. Before he could even finish his thought, Mr. Hip boomed once more ...

"If you're frustrated in your singleness, know that God has given you this gift in order to allow you to better focus on Him. If you stop focusing on dating and instead focus on serving God, He will lead you to marriage at the right time if that is His will for you."

As the speaker continued to highlight the spiritual benefits of singleness and point out the limitations to serving God once one was married, Mitch became convinced that it was not God's will for him to ask Misty out. If singleness was a gift from God, who was he to question it? Mitch quickly texted his wingman and called off the double-date. He slipped out during the last song, leaving behind a hurt and confused Misty. Mitch told himself it was for the best. He knew if he talked to her, he would lose his resolve. He went straight home, took a cold shower, and spent the rest of the evening reading Leviticus.

Can you identify with this scenario at all? Have you been shamed for wanting to be rid of your "gift"? Unfortunately, this doctrine has stood in the way of many marriage-minded singles, including myself, but that was about to change. Instead of continuing to accept PCC's message that my recently bestowed singleness was a gift, I decided to put all those expensive theology and hermeneutics classes to good use and dig into the scriptures myself. Allow me to walk you through my process.

The Mysterious Gift

The basis for the doctrine of the gift of singleness is the following passage from 1 Corinthians.

> I wish that all people were as I am. But each has his own gift from God, one person has this gift, another has that (*1 Corinthians 7:7*).

Popular Christian culture teaches that the unnamed gift in this verse refers to singleness. But does it?

Before we know how a passage applies to us today, we must first understand how it was understood by its original audience. This understanding can be obtained by studying its historical, cultural, and textual context. Context can usually be determined by asking the three Ws: who, why, and what. Let's begin.

1 Corinthians

(Note: Findings based on *The Historical Background of 1 Corinthians*[15])

1. Who wrote it?

   The author of 1 Corinthians is the apostle Paul.

2. Who was he writing to?

   The recipients were members of a church Paul had founded among the people of Corinth.

3. Who were the Corinthians?

   The Corinthians were a multinational Gentile (non-Jewish) congregation who had recently been converted to Christianity through Paul's preaching.

The Corinthians lived in the prosperous and influential city of Corinth. Corinth was known for its sexual licentiousness. They were so notorious that they became a Greek verb. "To Corinthianize" meant to make sexually immoral.[16] Their primary deity was Aphrodite, goddess of love. Her temple was the main attraction of the city. It was filled with over one thousand priestesses whose primary function was to prostitute themselves for the "worshipers."

To sum it up, the Corinthian's god was sex, their temple was a brothel, and their church service was an orgy. It kind of makes Las Vegas look like a blushing Southern belle, doesn't it?

---

[15] https://preachingsource.com/journal/the-historical-background-of-first-corinthians/

[16] https://www.biblica.com/resources/scholar-notes/niv-study-bible/intro-to-1-corinthians/

Keep this mental picture of the recipients in your mind, and let's ask some more questions.

4. Why was the letter written?

The purpose of the letter was twofold:

A. In chapters 1–6, Paul addressed and corrected behavioral issues within the congregation. One of his main concerns was the prevalence of sexual immorality (no surprise there).
B. In chapters 7–16, Paul responded to a series of questions concerning Christian life that the Corinthians had asked him about in a previous letter.

Now that we know the historical and cultural context of 1 Corinthians, we can better interpret the meaning of 1 Corinthians 7:7. Keep all this background information in mind as we ask our final question.

5. What is the topical context of 1 Corinthians 7:7?

As you can imagine, the chaste expectations of Christianity were entirely foreign to the Corinthians. As they tried to adjust, they ended up struggling with two extremes. Some believed their freedom in Christ meant they could continue to engage in complete sexual permissiveness. Paul vehemently opposed this view and admonished them to flee from sexual immorality. Unfortunately, this caused some in the congregation to overcorrect, and they began to teach that sexual relations were inherently evil and should be abstained from altogether, even within marriage.[17] The extreme abstinence adherents even coined their own slogan: "It is good for a man not to have sexual relations with a woman."

---

[17] https://thirdmill.org/seminary/lesson.asp/vid/8/version/

They shared this mantra with Paul in a letter they wrote to him and asked if they were now on the right track.

Unfortunately, to date, the letter the Corinthians wrote to Paul has since been lost to antiquity. However, Paul quotes part of it in his response letter to the Corinthian church. Paul's letter responding to the Corinthians' letter to him became known as the book in the Bible we now call 1 Corinthians.

> Now in response to the matters you wrote about: "It is good for a man not to have sexual relations with a woman." But because sexual immorality is so common, each man should have sexual relations with his own wife, and each woman should have sexual relations with her own husband. A husband should fulfill his marital duty to his wife and, likewise, a wife to her husband. A wife does not have the right over her own body, but her husband does. In the same way, a husband does not have the right over his own body, but his wife does. Do not deprive each other—except when you agree for a time to devote yourselves to prayer. Then come together again; otherwise, Satan may tempt you because of your lack of self-control. I say this as a concession, not as a command. I wish that all people were as I am. But each has his own gift from God, one person has this gift, another has that (*1 Corinthians 7:1–7*).

Instead of praising or agreeing with the extreme abstinence slogan, Paul counters it. Chastity within marriage does not guard against sexual immorality; it encourages it. To avoid sexual immorality, husbands and wives should have regular sex with each other. Therefore, Paul only approves of abstinence within marriage if it is brief and mutually agreed upon.

After clearing the issue up for the marrieds, Paul has a quick sex talk with the singles.

> I say to the unmarried and to widows: It is good for them if they remain as I am. But if they do not have self-control, they should marry, since it is better to marry than to burn with desire (*1 Corinthians 7:8–9*).

If the singles are OK with the required chastity that comes with their life stage, Paul says it is good for them to stay single. However, if they are struggling with sexual frustration, they should get married.

So far, I see nothing that would lead me to believe that the mysterious gift Paul is referring to in verse 7 is singleness. The context of the passage is all about the proper place of abstinence and sex within marriage. Also, 1 Corinthians 7:7 is within the section of the letter that is addressing married people. Paul doesn't address singles until verses 8–9, where he tells "the unmarried" to either zip it up or get hitched. Again, the context is regarding the proper context for sexual relations, not whether or not the single lifestyle is bestowed as a special gift from God

What then is this mysterious gift that Paul refers to? Since the topic of the passage is about abstinence and sex, I think it is most likely that his gift is the ability to remain celibate without struggling, thus enabling him to choose a single lifestyle without succumbing to temptation. However, Paul doesn't specify, so it is impossible to say for sure. And you know what? That's OK. We don't need to know what the gifts are to understand the overall meaning of the passage; abstinence is good but not within marriage. Sex is good but not outside of marriage.

How did a passage about the proper context for abstinence and sexual relations become the poster child for the gift of singleness? Just like last time, all roads lead back to the nineties. This time the path back takes us through the world of Bible translation.

A Tale of Three Bibles

There are three primary ways the Bible is translated from the original languages it was written into another language:

1. Word for word
2. Thought for thought
3. Paraphrase

Word for Word

The word-for-word translator endeavors to keep their interpretations to a bare minimum. They translate the words from the original text into the most accurate corresponding words in the new language. Of course, some interpretation while translating is necessary for clarity's sake. Still, any such altering of the exact words is kept as minimal as possible.

A word-for-word translation is like a Chick-fil-A (CFA) nugget. CFA nuggets are cut straight out of high-quality chicken breasts. No fillers, no chemicals, just meat. There's a reason why it's called God's chicken.

Thought for Thought

The thought-for-thought translator looks at the text in the original language, attempts to determine the author's thought (meaning), and then interprets that thought into the new language. A strictly thought-for-thought translation is considered less accurate than the word-for-word translation method. This is because the thought-for-thought method necessitates the translator to include more of their own interpretation of a passage before translating it.

A thought-for-thought translation is like the frozen chicken nuggets you buy at the grocery store. They have been ground up, processed, mixed with "other stuff," and even stamped into unnatural shapes. They are still meat, but all the tampering alters the taste and quality.

Paraphrase

The paraphrase translator is not a translator at all. Instead, they are readers who take a previously translated version of the Bible and then paraphrase what they read into their own words, usually with the intent of making the Bible more understandable. Because it is a rewording of a Bible translation, a paraphrase is not meant to be read authoritatively as God's Word. Instead, it is meant to be read and understood like a Bible commentary.

Think of a paraphrase like vegetarian chicken nuggets. They may look like the real thing, but there is not an ounce of chicken in them. I love vegetables in their proper context (a salad), but when they start masquerading as meat, I call foul (or not fowl in this case).

Thought-for-thought and paraphrase translations can be helpful when used to aid understanding. Still, they should always be used in conjunction with a word-for-word translation, especially if one is trying to establish sound doctrine.

The Living Bible

In the 1970s, a book was published by Tyndale called *The Living Bible* (TLB). It was the bestselling book in America between 1972 and 1973. *The Living Bible* was not a translation of the Bible but rather a paraphrase of the American Standard Version (ASV).

In *The Living Bible*, 1 Corinthians 7:7 reads differently[18]:

> I wish everyone could get along without marrying, just as I do. But we are not all the same. God gives some the gift of a husband or wife, and others he gives the gift of being able to stay happily unmarried (*1 Corinthians 7:7*, TLB).

As you can see, the verse now includes the concept that God gives marriage to some and singleness to others. The seed for the doctrine of the gift of singleness had been planted. However, it didn't blossom until about twenty years later.

In 1996 (see, I told you all roads lead back to the nineties), a revision to *The Living Bible* was published called the New Living Translation (NLT). The NLT had its own interpretation of 1 Corinthians 7:7, complete with a new catchphrase:

> I wish everyone could get along without marrying just as I do. But we are not all the same. God gives some the gift of marriage, and to others he gives *the gift of singleness* (*1 Corinthians 7:7 NLT*).

There you have it, ladies and gentlemen, the gift of singleness makes its debut. In a short period, 1 Corinthians went through quite a transformation. Let's do a quick recap before we go on. Below is a summary of the morphing of 1 Corinthians 7:7:

---

[18] https://betterbibles.wordpress.com/2008/01/02/the-gift-of-singleness/

Bible Translation	Year Published	Translation Method	1 Corinthians 7:7
American Standard Version (ASV)	1901	Word for word	Yet I would that all men were even as I myself. Howbeit each man hath his own gift from God, one after this manner, and another after that.
The Living Bible (TLB)	1971	Paraphrase	I wish everyone could get along without marrying, just as I do. But we are not all the same. God gives some the gift of a husband or wife, and others he gives *the gift of being able to stay happily unmarried.*
The New Living Translation (NLT)	1996	Thought for thought	I wish everyone could get along without marrying just as I do. But we are not all the same. God gives some the gift of marriage, and to others he gives *the gift of singleness.*

(Note: Later versions of the NLT removed the phrase "gift of singleness" from 1 Corinthians 7:7 and replaced the original ambiguity. It now reads "special gift.")

This explains where the gift of singleness came from, but how did it become such a mainstay of popular Christian culture's message to singles? Remember those culture-shifting Purity Prosperity Gospel books from the nineties that we went over in our "Merely Human Rules" chapter? Either the 1996 NLT and/ or *The Living Bible* are listed as the versions quoted and consulted in the making of the majority of them. That, my friends, is the story of the doctrine of the "gift of singleness."

What Now?

I had started out trying to better understand the gift of singleness and instead concluded that it was just another man-made doctrine that had been passed off as scriptural. I didn't know whether to be relieved or horrified.

If singleness was not a gift, then what was it?

I opened up my Bible and continued my investigation. I was pleasantly surprised to find that singleness was not a gift from God but rather a choice from God.

CHAPTER SIX

The Choice

The longer Andy remained single, the more he realized he liked it. The freedom to do his own thing, build his career, and socialize as little or as much as he wanted was quite liberating. Dating, love, and romance did not hold the appeal they once did. He was content. Sadly, others were not as happy with his life choices as he was.

> "You may not want companionship now, but you will be awfully lonely when you get older."
> —Dad (He tends to be a little needy.)
>
> "If you wait too long, all the good girls will be taken."
> —Mitch (Single best friend; how on earth would he know?)
>
> "Don't you ever want to have kids?"
> —Mom (She really needs littles to squeeze.)

Andy was secure in his decision, but all the concern from others had him wondering if they were right. Would he come to regret choosing singleness? Should he begin to seriously pursue marriage? After all, no one wants to be alone forever, do they?

Misty, on the other hand, had always dreamed of marriage. However, she had no success in dating and decided to serve God in singleness on the mission field. As she was preparing for life as a missionary, an old love interest showed up. She never thought she would see Mitch again after he ran out of singles group months ago. Now he was back and making his interest in dating her very clear. She told him that she was leaving soon to do missions. To her surprise, he shared that he also was seriously considering missions. "Why don't we go together?" he suggested.

Misty wants to say yes, but she feels guilty. She just surrendered her desire for marriage to pursue missions. She prayed and received no direct word to accept Mitch's offer. Does that mean that God wants her to say no and stay single?

Decisions, Decisions

The decision of whether to marry or remain single is a big one. I certainly struggled with it. I knew God had created marriage and called it good, but the Bible also had positive things to say about singleness. So how was I supposed to know which one was God's will for me?

Thankfully, I was not the first to face this dilemma. I remembered the Corinthians had also wondered which option was best, and thankfully, Paul had answered them. So I grabbed my Bible and opened it up to 1 Corinthians 7.

> Now about virgins: *I have no command from the Lord*, but I give a judgment as one who by the Lord's mercy is trustworthy ... I would like you to be free from concern. An unmarried man is concerned about the Lord's affairs—how he can

> please the Lord. But a married man is concerned about the affairs of this world—how he can please his wife—and his interests are divided. An unmarried woman or virgin is concerned about the Lord's affairs: Her aim is to be devoted to the Lord in both body and spirit. But a married woman is concerned about the affairs of this world—how she can please her husband. *I am saying this for your own good, not to restrict you,* but that you may live in a right way in undivided devotion to the Lord. But if a man thinks that he's treating his fiancée improperly and will inevitably give in to his passion, *let him marry her as he wishes.* It is not a sin. *But if he has decided firmly not to marry* and there is no urgency and he can control his passion, he does well not to marry (*1 Corinthians 7:25, 32–37 NIV;* emphasis added).

Paul says he has *no* direct word from God concerning whether or not to marry. Instead, he gives his judgment on the matter. Paul thinks singleness has many benefits, one being the ability to serve the Lord *single*-mindedly. In addition, the absence of the responsibilities of family life gives singles the ability to focus exclusively on the work of the ministry. For this reason, Paul preferred singleness and wished more people would follow in his footsteps. However, he stresses that his advocacy for the single life is not meant as a *restriction* on marriage (v. 35). Instead, Paul recommends marriage for those who *wish* to be married (v. 36) and singleness for those who *decide* to be single (v. 37).

Say whaaaat?! Do people get to choose? I was taught that God did the choosing and people did the accepting. This couldn't possibly be right. I had better get a second opinion.

Paul had the most to say regarding marriage and singleness, but Jesus also spoke on the topic.

In Matthew 19:11–12, Jesus was being questioned by religious leaders, Pharisees, hoping to discredit Him. Their most recent interrogation was regarding the Mosaic laws concerning divorce. Jesus denounced the law that permitted them to divorce for *any* reason. Instead, He declared that divorce for any reason, *except* infidelity, was invalid, and remarriage, after such a divorce, was adulterous. His disciples were startled by His strict standard and declared,

> "If the relationship of a man with his wife is like this, it's better not to marry." He (Jesus) responded, "Not everyone can accept this saying, but only those to whom it has been given. For there are eunuchs who were born that way from their mother's womb, there are eunuchs who were made by men, and there are eunuchs who have made themselves that way because of the kingdom of heaven. The one who is able to accept it should accept it" (*Matthew 19:10–14*).

Jesus, like Paul, acknowledged that not everyone could accept the celibate/single life. He described three categories of people for whom celibacy was the necessary or preferred option:

1. Those born unable to have sexual relations for various reasons.
2. Those forcibly castrated by others.
3. Those who voluntarily choose celibacy/singleness so that they can serve God with the benefits particular to that lifestyle.

Jesus, like Paul, described voluntary singleness as an intentional choice made by the individual.

Called to Singleness?

All this reading and I still had yet to find any examples of God choosing the life of singleness for anyone. So I decided to take a technological shortcut. When all else fails, Google it, right? I typed "Did God command anyone to stay single?" into my search bar. I expected a list, but only one name popped up—Jeremiah, the weeping prophet. I didn't recall required singleness being a part of Jeremiah's story, so I reread it.

Poor Jeremiah was handed a truly difficult assignment from God. He was called to prophesy to Israel of their impending doom once their wickedness had reached the point of no return. Not only that, but also God even told him that his ministry would be completely unsuccessful. On top of all that, God also commanded Jeremiah not to marry. No wonder the poor guy was always crying.

> The word of the Lord came to me: "Do not marry
> or have sons or daughters in this place" (*Jeremiah
> 16:1–2*).

God went on to explain that the reason Jeremiah must not marry was because of the great judgment that was coming upon His nation. God did not want Jeremiah to start a family under such conditions.

Popular Christian culture teaches that everyone is called to singleness until the Lord calls them to marry. However, according to the Bible, marriage is something that singles may choose at their discretion *unless* God specifically commands them not to. In other words, if you receive a lightning bolt to the backside coupled with a booming voice instructing you to never marry, you are probably called to singleness. However, if you receive no such direct command, you have God's permission to choose either singleness or marriage at your own discretion. No seeking of divine revelation is required.

This means that Misty does not need a personal word from God to accept Mitch's offer. God has already made it clear in His written Word that those who wish to marry should do so (1 Corinthians 7:9, 7:36). Misty's desire for companionship and love is natural and God-given. She needn't feel guilty for pursuing the God-ordained relationship of marriage to fulfill those longings. God created marriage and called it good. No other opinion is necessary.

On the flip side, Andy is under no biblical obligation to marry. His lack of desire for wedlock indicates that he should not pursue it. He needn't feel that anything is wrong with him, worry that he is missing out, or fear that he will one day regret forgoing marriage. God Himself says that singleness is a good choice. No other opinion is needed. Andy is free to choose the benefits of singleness for as long as he wants. His decision is not permanent or indicative of a lifelong "call" to singleness. He may choose singleness for a time and then later decide if he wants to marry. Paul himself was clear that his choice to remain single did not infringe on his right to marry someday if he chose.

> Don't we have the right to be accompanied by a believing wife like the other apostles, the Lord's brothers, and Cephas? (*1 Corinthians 9:5*) ❧

One may initially choose a life of singleness and then later decide they would prefer to be married. Until now, I have only told you of my struggle with singleness, but there was a time in my life when I preferred it. I knew of the spiritual benefits of singleness and determined that I wanted to use those to better serve the Lord. I also had educational and personal desires that I wanted to pursue without the responsibilities and limitations that come with marriage and a family. I did not desire marriage and was not struggling with sexual temptation. Those years of singleness were a choice, but as we all know, a woman reserves the right to change her mind.

You are at a fork in the road, my friend. God has given you the responsibility to choose what relational state you wish to serve Him in—marriage or singleness. Both choices are good, both have their benefits and drawbacks, and both can be used mightily by God. Take some time to reflect, weigh the pros and cons, and make your choice. If you choose marriage, know this: The journey to matrimony begins with choosing; it does not end here.

CHAPTER SEVEN

The Prerequisite

One of my pet peeves in college was that pesky little thing known as a prerequisite. I always had to pass some lame preliminary course to get to the good stuff. One, in particular, cramped my style. I needed a second science to complete my degree. I looked over the catalog and was excited to see Genetics 101. The prerequisite was Biology 101. According to the course description, it was exactly like the Introduction to Biology class I had already taken at a community college. I decided to petition the university to accept my Intro-to-Biology credit and allow me to bypass Bio 101. To my surprise, the head of the science department requested a meeting with me. He was a middle-aged man who looked a little like Colonel Sanders from KFC. I walked into his office armed with a recommendation letter and youthful ignorance. He didn't even get up or ask me to sit down. Instead, he glared at me through slitted eyes and declared, "Miss, there is no way your community college course is on par with this department's Bio 101. You are not qualified to enroll in Genetics 101."

Not to be deterred, I responded, "But I am really good in science. I have a recommendation letter from—"

Suddenly, Colonel Sanders went nuclear. "Who did you think you are?!" he shrieked with blazing eyes as he lurched forward in his desk chair. "This university's science department is state of the art! How dare you think you have what it takes to bypass our prerequisites!"

I excused myself and scurried out of there, thanking God that I was not a science major.

Thankfully, missing out on genetics would not affect my life in the long term. However, years later, I would come against a different type of prerequisite that would put my life on hold.

Contentment 101

As I tried to figure out the route from singleness to matrimony, I decided to consult a recently married friend. She must know the secret to getting out of singleness. But to my dismay, instead of giving me a map, she threw up a roadblock.

"God brought me my husband when I finally stopped looking and learned to be content with just Him," she confided. "When you learn to find satisfaction in singleness, God will send you a spouse as He did for me."

Sigh … Here we go again. It wasn't the first time I had been told that my longing for marriage was the very thing keeping me from it. For years, I had tried to be satisfied just in my relationship with God. Yet regardless of how close God and I were, there was always a specific longing inside of me for the companionship of a spouse. I couldn't turn it off.

Why couldn't I reach the required singleness nirvana that she had? But then again, wasn't the ring on her finger evidence that she was not as satisfied in singleness as she thought? What did it even look like to be truly content?

Baby Blue

When I was a young professional, my first big purchase was a used royal blue Honda Fit. I loved that car and was super proud of it. I dubbed her Baby Blue. We were the perfect "fit" for each other. She was a little rough around the edges, but she was mine. One day I took her to the Honda dealership to have some minor repair work done. While waiting, a salesman approached and asked if I was there for a new ride.

"No, I'm just here getting my Fit worked on," I responded.

"You don't want that old thing anymore," he said with disgust. "I've got some new arrivals you're going to just love."

Did this guy seriously just diss my beloved car?

"No, thank you," I said as my stance and tone stiffened. "I like my Fit."

"You like Fits?" he went on, completely undeterred. "We've got some brand new Fits right over here. We'll trade your basic model in today and get you a *real* car."

That's it! He just crossed the line. "Quit trashing on my car, mister!" I retorted as I stomped my foot and folded my arms. "I wouldn't trade Baby Blue for one of your Fits for any amount of money."

He apologized and quickly scurried off, muttering something about never having met someone who truly didn't want a new car.

I rejected the offer of a new ride because I was content with what I had.

Wouldn't genuinely content singles spurn marriage just like I had rejected those Fits?

Why did people who chose marriage feel the need to credit their wedded bliss to having achieved contentment without it?

It just didn't make any sense.

Where did the idea of the contentment prerequisite come from?

I typed "contentment in singleness" into my search bar. My

browser was flooded with articles touting the familiar mantra. Here is a sampling.

"There's a solution for your heartache … Your deepest desire may be to find the one. Except, you've already found 'the one.' His name is Jesus."[19]

"If you are not content in singleness, you will not be content in marriage."[20]

"If you have struggled with frustration over your singleness, be encouraged that contentment and joy in this season of your life are possible—but only when you become secure in Jesus."[21]

Apparently, it is more righteous to suffer well in singleness than try to do anything about it.

I had committed not to take anyone's word for it regarding sound biblical doctrine, and the contentment prerequisite was no exception. I identified the top 3 scriptures that popular Christian culture uses to support the contentment-in-God-alone prerequisite and started reading.

I have learned to be content in whatever circumstances I find myself (*Philippians 4:11*).

But godliness with contentment is great gain (*1 Timothy 6:6*).

Keep your life free from the love of money. Be satisfied with what you have, for he himself has said, I will never leave you or abandon you (*Hebrews 13:5*).

As always, context is key. A little research revealed that the

---

[19] https://writingforjesus.com/godly-advice-for-singles-its-not-a-curse
[20] https://waitingforyourboaz.com/if-you-are-not-content-being-single-you-will-not-be-content-in-marriage
[21] https://setapartgirl.com/contentment-singleness/

topical context of these primary texts is being satisfied/content with one's material possessions. None have anything to do with one's relationship state.

I searched the Bible cover to cover and could not find anywhere where people are either commanded or encouraged to be content relationally in God alone. In fact, the very first marriage began because God declared that having Him alone was not good.

Marriage 101

Day 6 dawned on a perfect world. God had made so many wonderful things. There were limitless galaxies, a striking landscape, and countless fantastic animals to bear witness to the creativity of the Creator. God wowed the world once more by creating a creature in His very own image. He called it a man. Up until this point, God said that everything He had made was very good.

Then something strange happened. For the first time, the Lord declared that something within creation was not good.

> Then the LORD God said, "It is not good for the man to be alone … (*Genesis 2:18*)

And all the lonely singles said, "AMEN!"

I noticed for the first time that Adam was not alone. He had God Himself as his companion. Yet God determined that something, or rather someone, was still lacking.

> So God declares, "I will make a helper corresponding to him" (*Genesis 2:18*).

Then the Lord did something strange. Instead of just whipping up a mate for Adam, He presented him with all the other creatures on the planet for him to choose a mate from.

> The man gave names to all the livestock, to the birds of the sky, and to every wild animal; but for the man no helper was found corresponding to him (*Genesis 2:20*).

Poor Adam had just been introduced to every other living thing on earth, and none were a match for him. Dogs may be man's best friend, but for some reason, Fido just wasn't cutting it for Adam. There was an ache in his heart, and he didn't even know what for. Why would the Lord make Adam's aloneness so painfully obvious to him? I think it was because God knew he needed to feel the longing to appreciate the provision.

> So the Lord God caused a deep sleep to come over the man, and he slept. God took one of his ribs and closed the flesh at that place. Then the Lord God made the rib he had taken from the man into a woman and brought her to the man (*Genesis 2:21–22*).

Adam was so overcome with emotion when he saw the woman that he broke into poetry.

> *This one*, at last, is bone of my bone and flesh of my flesh; this one will be called "woman," for she was taken from man (*Genesis 2:23*; emphasis added).

Adam was no longer alone. He had a mate. He knew instinctively that this new creature had come from him, so he named her woman. The narrator goes on to tell us that this beautiful story is the reason for marriage.

This is why a man leaves his father and mother and bonds with his wife, and they become one flesh (*Genesis 2:24*).

Man and woman desire to join together in body, mind, and soul within a marriage covenant because they are innately linked to each other. Fire and heat, ice and cold, peanut butter and jelly—some things just intrinsically belong together. Man and woman were made to love each other because their Creator designed it that way.

Rereading the story of the first marriage forever changed my perspective on God's attitude toward my heart's cry for love. The same God who noticed Adam's loneliness saw my pain as well. He did not selfishly withhold a mate from Adam until he learned to be content without one, and He was not withholding love from me either. The divine remedy for human loneliness was the provision of an intimate relationship with another person.

This story is a perfect example of what the Bible teaches about God's role in human needs. Scripture teaches that God will *provide*, not *be*, all that we need.

And my God will supply all your needs according to his riches in glory in Christ Jesus (*Philippians 4:19*).

All eyes look to you, and you give them their food at the proper time. You open your hand and satisfy the desire of every living thing (*Psalm 145:15–16*).

Don't strive for what you should eat and what you should drink, and don't be anxious. For the Gentile world eagerly seeks all these things, and your Father knows that you need them. But seek

> his kingdom, and these things will be provided for you (*Luke 12:29–31*).

God is the source of life, so He could have chosen to sustain people directly with only Himself, but He didn't. Instead, God designed people as physical beings with physical needs, and these scriptures attest that God will provide for these needs. God also designed people as relational beings with relational needs. This can be seen through the two greatest commandments:

> Love the Lord your God with all your heart, with all your soul, and with all your mind. This is the greatest and most important command. The second is like it: Love your neighbor as yourself (*Matthew 22:37–39*).

We are commanded to love God *and* love our neighbor. This is because God designed people to have relationships with other people. We were not made to be satisfied in our relationship with God alone. Instead, we were made to crave and pursue relationships with others, and for some of us, that includes a spouse.

Popular Christian culture's demand that singles learn to be content in God alone before marriage is not only unbiblical, but it is also detrimental. Telling a single struggling with loneliness that they should be satisfied with God is like telling a starving person that their relationship with God should satisfy their hunger. The starving person has a legitimate need for food, and the lonely single has a legitimate need for companionship. Marriage-minded singles are not going to be content in singleness. Insisting that they learn to be happy alone sets them up for failure and frustration.

Hear me, friend. Being sick of singleness does not make you less spiritual—it makes you human. God is not disappointed in you for not being satisfied with just Him because He never meant for you to be. God designed you for companionship.

> It is not good for the man to be alone. I will make a helper corresponding to him (*Genesis 2:18*).

God says that people are better together.

> Two are better than one because they have a good reward for their efforts. For if either falls, his companion can lift him up; but pity the one who falls without another to lift him up. (*Ecclesiastes 4:9–10*).

God's heart toward human loneliness is to relieve it.

> God sets the lonely in families (*Psalm 68:6*).

It is time to change the narrative. Singleness is not a divine boot camp that trains people to find their satisfaction in God alone. It is merely a stage of life that we all start in and are free to leave if and when we so desire.

Discontentment in singleness does not disqualify singles for marriage; instead, it is the motivation that spurs them toward it. Are you sick of singleness? Then take it as a sign that it is time to pull off Highway I-Solo and merge onto Highway I-Duo. However, I must warn you that the route can be a little rough at times. The next roadblock is a real doozie.

CHAPTER EIGHT

The Wait

Andy was one of the most eligible bachelors in the singles group. He was handsome, talented, charming, and best of all, he loved Jesus. Although he was a great catch, Andy hadn't had a serious relationship for some time. The break had been by choice, but now he found himself wanting to be in a relationship. He expressed frustration to a friend one night that it didn't seem like there were any good girls left. She told him that he needed to start looking if he expected to find someone. Her advice was met with immediate objections by others in their social circle.

> Friend 1: "Pray and *wait* on the Lord, Andy!"

> Friend 2: "Yeah, if you try to make it happen, you will get ahead of God."

> Friend 3: "Have faith and *wait* for God's timing. Don't take matters into your own hands."

Have you been told similar things? I sure was. The necessity to passively "wait" was preached to me from all corners of Christianity during my single years. I spent countless nights tearfully crying out to God to send me a spouse and received nothing. I blamed myself for being impatient, not being content, and not having enough faith. I felt trapped. I felt like I was a prisoner of waiting. Can you identify with this? Have you felt trapped in a cycle of waiting that just won't end?

Of all the doctrines that hinder marriage, the misapplication of "wait on the Lord" has claimed the most hostages. Unlike the previous two doctrines we tackled, the admonition to "wait on the Lord" is all over the Bible. It typically denotes an attitude of anticipation and expectation of God's provision/deliverance.[22] This understanding is very applicable in the context of dating and marriage. However, the popular understanding of "wait on the Lord" has moved away from an *attitude* of trust to a *position* of passivity. Christian singles are told that they must wait on God to provide them with a compatible person. The belief is that asking and then passively waiting is a sign of faith, while actively seeking is a sign of doubt. During my season of unwanted singleness, I was advised to pray "trusting" prayers like this:

"Please, God, if it's Your will, send me a spouse but only in Your timing. I trust Your perfect plan for me. I only want what You want."

Have you been coached to approach God like this? I don't know about you, but every time I prayed those things, I wasn't being completely genuine. Although I did long to please and serve God with my life, I also desperately wanted someone to do it with. I felt that if I was honest with God about the depth of my need and desire, He would see it as a lack of faith. So I continued to wait and pray anemic prayers until one day God showed me what real prayer and biblical waiting were supposed to look like.

I was reading the familiar passage where Jesus's disciples asked Him to teach them to pray. He told them a parable of a

---

[22] https://www.biblestudytools.com/encyclopedias/isbe/wait.html

man who went to a friend's house asking for bread in the middle of the night. At first, the friend brushed him off, but he eventually gave in because of the man's relentlessness. According to Jesus, this man's tenacity illustrates the attitude we should bring when we have a request from God.

> So I say to you, Ask and it will be given to you. Seek, and you will find. Knock, and the door will be opened to you. For everyone who asks, receives, and the one who seeks, finds, and to the one who knocks, the door will be opened (*Luke 11:9–10*).

I had read this story countless times, but now the three action words stuck out to me: ask, seek, and knock. It was almost like a step-by-step formula. I knew Jesus was talking about prayer, but I thought prayer stopped at asking. What did Jesus mean?

Ask = Receive

Whenever I try to interpret a passage, I often find it helpful to do a word study on both the translated and original languages.[23] Therefore, we will look closer at each action word in this prayer formula to learn how to apply it.

> *Ask* (verb): to request someone to do or give something.
> *Synonyms*: request, beg, plead, or call for.
> *Antonyms*: tell, insist, or demand.

In this passage, the word *ask* is translated from the Greek word

---

[23] To study the original Greek or Hebrew, I use the Blue Letter Bible Lexicon found at blueletterbible.org.

aiteō.[24] It suggests a humble supplication made by a subordinate to their superior. The asker recognizes who they are in relation to God and approaches Him accordingly.

I recalled a story later in Luke about a blind man who modeled asking with the relentlessness of the friend from the parable.

The blind man's name was Bartimaeus. He was sitting by the side of the road, begging when he heard a vast crowd approaching. Puzzled, he asked what was going on. Jesus of Nazareth was coming! The man who had given others their sight would be within his reach. Jesus was the blind man's only hope of ever being able to see. What did Bartimaeus do? Did he pray and wait? No, he began to call out loudly, "Jesus! Son of David! Have mercy on me!"

The crowd told him to be quiet. He wasn't discouraged. Being shushed only made him call out louder.

"Jesus! Son of David! Have mercy on me!"

What did Jesus do? Did He tell him to wait and trust in God's timing? No, Jesus stopped the entire caravan and gave the blind man His full attention.

He asked him, "What do you want me to do for you?"

"Lord," he said, "I want to see."

> "Receive your sight," Jesus told him. "Your faith has saved you." Instantly, he could see, and he began to follow him ... (*Luke 18:40–42*).

The blind man's faith was displayed through activity, not passivity. Jesus's heart was moved, not by a halfhearted request but by desperate pleading.

Is your heart crying out for someone to share your life with? Then don't approach God with anemic *only-help-me-if-You-want-to* prayers. God already knows what you are thinking and

---

[24] https://www.blueletterbible.org/lexicon/g154/csb/mgnt/0-1/

feeling, so tell Him. We get God's attention through honesty, not complacency.

Seek and You Will Find

The second step in Jesus's prayer formula is to seek. What does it mean to seek?

> *Seek* (verb): to go in search or quest of, to try to find, or to try to obtain.
> *Synonyms*: explore, follow, investigate, or pursue.
> *Antonyms*: ignore, avoid, relinquish, or disregard.

The word *seek* is translated from the Greek word *zēteō*.[25] It means to seek earnestly and tenaciously with the intent to find. It means to exert every effort toward obtaining what is sought after. It denotes a stance that is completely opposite of the "wait on the Lord" doctrine. This kind of seeking is the epitome of taking matters into your own hands.

This step in the prayer formula was the most puzzling for me. I could not fathom what such seeking would look like in terms of the search for a spouse. Fortunately for me, God sent a new friend whose love story was a perfect example.

When I met Cory and Josi, I was immediately struck by what a fantastic couple they were. They seemed like such a good fit for each other. Of course, being the hopeless romantic that I am, I was eager to learn how this match began. To my great surprise, Josi nonchalantly informed me that they met on the dating site Christian Mingle.

"Wait … what?" My tone was playfully incredulous. "You met your husband by actually *trying* to find him? I didn't know that was allowed. Weren't you afraid you were getting ahead of God?"

---

[25] https://www.blueletterbible.org/lexicon/g2212/csb/mgnt/0-1/

"Well," she replied, "I just prayed and told God I had this desire, and I was going to pursue it. If what I was doing was wrong, I asked him to show me."

Intrigued, I asked her to share more of her story.

She had been longing for a husband and had received the typical "pray and wait on the Lord" advice. She did some soul-searching as well as some searching of the scriptures. She determined that there was no biblical mandate that she wait passively for God to bring her a husband. She believed that her desire for a mate was from God, so she began to do everything in her power to find one.

She joined church singles groups, opened accounts on three dating sites, and even joined a singles adventure group. If there was a wholesome way to find a spouse, this girl did it. Her approach might seem a little extreme, but the Bible shares a similar story of a match made through intentional, focused effort.

When Abraham's miracle son, Isaac, needed a wife, Abraham did not sit around waiting for another miracle. Instead, he sent his head servant on a *two-thousand*-mile quest to find one. God did not chide Abraham for "taking matters into his own hands." Instead, He prospered Abraham's efforts and led the servant to Rebecca, a compatible woman willing to leave everything for a husband she had never seen (Genesis 24).

This is what it looks like to biblically seek. Prayer does not stop at asking. The next step is getting up and going after what you are praying for.

Don't worry about "getting ahead of God." A measly human cannot thwart Almighty God. On the contrary, He declares that His will is absolute.

> Remember what happened long ago,
> for I am God, and there is no other;
> I am God, and no one is like me.
> I declare the end from the beginning,

and from long ago what is not yet done,
saying: my plan *will* take place,
and I *will do* all my will …
Yes, I have spoken; so I will also bring it about.
I have planned it; I will also do it (*Isaiah 46:9–11*;
emphasis added).

God isn't worried about being overtaken by your romantic pursuits, so get busy and put some legs on those prayers! There is no sin in seeking.

If you have already been seeking diligently and are still coming up empty-handed, then we need to talk strategy. No amount of seeking will help you if you are searching in the wrong place. High-quality spouses are scarce; even the Bible says so. It likens them to treasure and priceless jewels. To find treasure, you have to know where to look.

> Do you want someone godly? Then go to God's house.
> Do you want someone smart? Go to a university.
> Do you want someone willing to invest in a relationship? Use free dating sites with caution; remember, you get what you pay for.

If you've been looking in all the "right" places and still not getting anywhere, then it's time to broaden your search. In the words of a wise man, "If you keep fishing in the same shallow pond, don't blame it on the fish."

I attended a small church while in college. We had no designated singles group, so the lone single career woman, Kim, was stuck with us, college kids. She certainly had no prospects in our church, and her current social circle wasn't looking too good either. Our Sunday school teacher finally suggested Kim start attending a different church. Gasp! Kim was shocked at the suggestion. She had grown up in this congregation. Visiting a different church was unthinkable.

Her hesitancy was understandable. Churches can be very possessive of their members. Voluntarily joining another congregation may as well be treason. Kim held on as long as she could, but eventually, the *desperada* bailed ship. Do you know what happened? She clicked with a guy in the first church she visited, and within a year, she was engaged.

Seek, my friend, and if your efforts bring you to what appears to be a closed door, instead of giving up, knock.

Knock until the Door Opens

The final step in the prayer formula is to knock.

> *Knock* (verb): to strike or hit heavily and repeatedly.
> *Synonyms*: tap, rap, bang, or pound.
> *Antonyms*: be still, give up, or surrender.

The Greek word translated as *knock* is *krouō*.[26] It denotes a continuous, relentless knocking.

Jesus illustrated how this step applies to prayer in the parable of the persistent widow.

> Now he told them a parable on the need for them to pray always and not give up. "There was a judge in a certain town who didn't fear God or respect people. And a widow in that town kept coming to him, saying, "Give me justice against my adversary." For a while, he was unwilling, but later he said to himself, "Even though I don't fear God or respect people, yet because this widow

---

[26] https://www.blueletterbible.org/lexicon/g2925/csb/mgnt/0-1/

keeps pestering me, I will give her justice so that
she doesn't wear me out by her persistent coming"
(*Luke 18:1–5*).

Jesus went on to say that if such persistence was effective with
an unjust, uncaring judge, how much more effective will it be
with a caring, just God! Genuine faith is not asking and waiting.
Genuine faith is asking, seeking, knocking ... asking, seeking,
knocking ... asking, seeking, knocking ... until the door opens.
The road to success is paved with persistence.

Have I convinced you to take an active role in your love life? I
hope so because now I am going to tell you how to wait.

Necessary Interval

We just spent this whole chapter breaking free, and here I am
using that nasty four-letter word again. I'm not asking you to
go back to being a prisoner of waiting. Instead, I'm encouraging
you to partner with waiting. Regardless of how you conduct your
spousal search, some amount of waiting will be involved. There
is a natural interval between asking and receiving, seeking and
finding, knocking and the door being opened. This interval is
when you must wait.

Just be sure you are waiting actively instead of passively.
Passive waiting sits around and expects a handout. Active waiting
contributes to the process through anticipation, preparation, and
participation.

When I was a nanny, one of my biggest pet peeves was when
the kids would stand around waiting to be served at dinnertime.

"Please find something to do," I would say.

"What can we do?"

"You can anticipate your need for plates and set the table.
Prepare yourself for dinner and wash your hands. Participate by
helping me carry the food to the table."

Stay busy during the waiting. Anticipate your future needs as a spouse and prepare for them. Pursue an education or a career. Participate in life and grow as a person. Make meaningful friendships. One of them might even turn into something more. When you make the most of the necessary intervals, they become more bearable.

I wish I could say I eagerly and immediately applied the breakthrough prayer formula I just shared with you, but I didn't. The wait on the Lord doctrine had a cultural partner in crime that had to be dealt with before I could fully break free.

PART 3

CULTURAL HINDRANCES

Societal Expectations That Prolong Singleness

CHAPTER NINE

Romance by Happenstance

I was waiting in the seminary cafeteria checkout line when I realized I had forgotten to grab a fork. I awkwardly bumbled out of line, trying not to spill my tray or take anyone out with my rollie backpack. Finally, I grabbed a fork and got back in line, only to drop it. I sighed and stared at the elusive eating utensil in defeat, ready to just give up and eat with my hands. Then I heard a chuckle and looked up. A handsome man with sky blue eyes and wavy sandy-blond hair was grinning at me, holding out a fork.

"Here you go, ma'am," he said in a deep Southern drawl.

"Thank you," I said as a fierce blush climbed up my cheeks.

I would have to make a clumsy fool of myself in front of the preacher-boy version of Matthew McConaughey.

"I see you like coffee," Mr. Charming drawled again.

I looked at my collection of coffee cups on my tray and blushed even deeper. Don't judge me. You know those silly little Styrofoam cups don't hold more than a sip.

"We should do Starbucks together sometime," he practically purred. "Here's my number."

75

Wow! If I had known that dropping things around here led to dates, I would have thrown my whole tray on the floor long ago.

"I'm free tomorrow," I purred back, kicking my own Southern drawl into overdrive. I was actually free right then and there, but I didn't want to look desperate.

We went on the standard coffee predate the following day. Seminarians have a tight budget. The coffee predate allows them to ensure the girl is a good prospect before investing a real dinner in the relationship. I must have passed the test because he asked me out to dinner afterward.

Sadly, although our meet-cute[27] had all the makings of the perfect Hallmark movie, our relationship was clunky at best. I didn't want to go back to throwing forks on the floor, so I stuck it out for a while, hoping things would get better, but we just weren't a good fit.

I felt so discouraged. Ricky and I had broken up over a year before, and Mr. Charming was the only opportunity I had had to date since then.

I wonder how long I will have to wait for another chance meeting with a cute guy this time?

The American culture's romance script is all about the chance encounter. From kindergarten to adulthood, love is portrayed as something that just happens. I recalled the first experience I had with romance. I was five years old, watching Disney's *Beauty and the Beast* in a movie theater. Belle and the Beast had been brought together through extraordinary, unplanned circumstances, and love had grown between them as if by magic.

My teenage self was equally taken with Elisabeth Bennet and Mr. Darcy's happenstance romance in the classic *Pride and Prejudice*. The two initially disdained each other, but fate continued to throw them together until they learned to love each other.

---

[27] Meet-cute: a happenstance meeting that usually occurs cutely or amusingly between two people who are destined to fall in love.

In my college years, popular Christian culture encouraged the cultural expectation of romance by happenstance. For example, have you heard the illustration of "the marathon runner"? It goes something like this:

"If you're wondering how to meet someone to do life with who loves God as you do, then just start running hard after God. As you're running, look around at the people running alongside you headed toward the same goal. These are the people you will want to team up with in life."

It sounded so spiritual, even practical, until I tried it. I had been running hard after God for years, and the only runners who "happened" to come alongside me and offer a relationship turned out to be poor running mates at best and full-on disasters at worst.

Secular culture called upon fate, and Christian culture called upon God, but regardless of the source, the message was the same—romance was something you *happened upon,* and love was something you *fell into.*

I had held out for this love story script for so long that I was having a hard time accepting that it simply wasn't working for me. I wanted that whimsical meet-cute story. I wanted the romance of the chance encounter. I wanted the American love story. Even if it turned out to be nothing more than a dream, I wasn't ready to wake up until Bhavik had to come along and sink my dream boat.

Bhavik was an Indian pastor friend who found the fact that I was still single very disconcerting.

"Why aren't you married?" he sprang on me one day.

"I ... I don't know," I stammered. "I guess I just haven't met the right one yet."

He shook his head regretfully. "That's why you're not married. Waiting around for a match to come to you is the American way, and it doesn't work. In India, we don't wait for a match to just happen—we make the match. Parents introduce good matches to children, and if they like the match, we pray and fast for a week, and then they get married."

"That's very efficient," I admitted.

"Don't do it the American way anymore. Come to India! We'll get you a good husband!" he declared with fatherly determination.

In my younger years, I would have been utterly appalled by the suggestion of an arranged marriage, but now I seriously considered taking him up on that offer. I certainly wasn't getting anywhere with the "American" way.

The truth was that both secular and Christian cultures' portrayal and expectations of romance contributed to my stint in prolonged singleness. Chance and fate were terrible matchmakers. Running after God and expecting Mr. Right to just show up alongside me was about as productive as running past a grocery store and expecting a meal to appear.

Happenstance romance may have been relatively plentiful when most of my peers were single and ready to mingle, but now most of them were taken; there ain't no mistaken. Even if I was lucky enough to spill coffee on a cute guy "Hallmark style," he would probably be married with several kids, and the only reason he would want my number would be to forward the dry-cleaning bill.

The time had come to face the facts. I could either continue to hold out for the way it was "supposed to happen" or switch tactics. Just because my dating pool had turned into a muddy puddle didn't mean I had to keep fishing in it. It was time to take my rod and reel elsewhere. I didn't want to throw in the towel entirely and accept Bhavik's offer just yet, so I started looking for less drastic options.

God said to seek and you will find, so maybe I should try going full-on Sherlock.

"Where do I start the search, Lord?" I asked enthusiastically.

His answer made me wish I had just gone with the arranged marriage.

The Dreaded Door

I stood outside the door and tried to work up the courage to walk in.

I can leave now, and no one would know I was here. I can just go home and watch a chick flick.

God: "There are no potential matches in your flat screen."

I can go home and have another quiet time, Lord, You know, pray for my future husband.

God: "Seeking is a part of prayer."

I could keep seeking at school. I saw a cute new guy just last week. He might be single.

God: "Open the door and go in."

*Please, God! There must be another way! Please don't make me go to a—*gulp*—church singles group.*

Sigh … If you weren't already well aware of your relational status, you will be after the church slaps a big available sign across your chest in the form of a nametag, your name written in all caps, in black sharpie. They may as well call it the failure-to-launch group, the marital-rejects class, or lonely hearts anonymous. The somber setting, the complete lack of opportunity for interaction, and the consistent theme of finding contentment in singleness can make some such groups feel like relational timeout.

Thankfully, many congregations have seen the need for a different approach and have scrapped the drab timeout routine in favor of a lively model that encourages natural connections. When done well, singles groups can be a very effective way to grow your dating pool and make meaningful connections. The group I joined catered in popular restaurants, hosted games and parties, and enlisted a connections team to facilitate community. It turned out to be quite the social hub and eventually became one of the highlights of my week. I made many friends and even went on a few dates.

Sadly, even though I was getting more bites, I still hadn't found one I could reel in. I had finally committed to applying the prayer formula wholeheartedly, so I began searching for how to broaden my horizons once more. My next adventure took the pond and turned it into an ocean.

The Final Frontier

My least desired avenue to seek a mate was finally knocking at my door in the form of Josi's incessant pestering.

"You need to try online dating! It's a great way to meet new people. That's how Cory and I met …"

How could I ever forget? Online dating platforms should give you a cut for all the promoting you do.

I didn't even want to pray that night. I knew what God was going to tell me. But as I sat on a bench in the seminary gardens and finally began my nightly prayer time, I felt a peace wash over me. It was going to be OK. I had avoided it long enough. It was time to face the final frontier.

I didn't want to do it alone, so I decided to ask my roommate to join me. I was working up the nerve to ask her when I awoke to a loud banging one morning.

Bang! The bedroom door slammed.
Bang! The kitchen cabinet shut.
Bang! The cereal bowl hit the counter

"You OK?" I asked as I tiptoed gingerly into the kitchen.

"You know those friends who were encouraging me to sign up for eHarmony?" she spat out, eyes blazing. "Well, they decided not to take *no* for an answer. They signed me up last night without telling me. I woke up to dozens of e-mails telling me to check out my new matches."

"Seriously?" I snorted while choking back laughter. This was too funny.

Her voice rose to a shriek. "Guess who my first match is?! Mr. Hipster!"

What were the chances?! Mr. Hipster was a member of roomie's small group at church. He was the quintessential hipster, complete with a man bun and epically long beard. Poor guy had been trying to get roomie's attention for months. Sadly, the feelings were not mutual, and she had successfully dodged his efforts until now! This whole thing was playing out like a rom-com. I considered grabbing some popcorn and enjoying the show.

"What am I going to do?" she said in dismay. "He'll have seen the 'match' by now too. I don't have the heart to tell him the profile was fake. I'll have to switch churches. I might have to change my name!"

With that, she threw the sofa blanket over her head and collapsed among the pillows in defeat. Thespians, gotta love 'em.

I decided to put off asking her to join me in my online dating adventure until the Mr. Hipster fiasco died down a bit. After a few weeks, I felt the time was right to strike.

"Let's try online dating together!" I exclaimed in a chipper tone one evening.

She slowly lowered her World Missions textbook just enough to glare at me with squinted eyes.

I quickly pleaded my case lest she kill me with that stare. "The reason why you were matched with 'you know who' is because they signed you up as a joke. It will be different this time. Come on, what have we got to lose?"

My powers of persuasion must be second to none because she eventually agreed. We sat on opposite ends of the sofa and each filled out dating sites' *super romantic* extensive questionnaire.

1. Do you want children?
2. Are you comfortable dating someone who has been divorced?
3. What is your desired age range for a spouse?
4. What, if any, are your religious affiliations?

As I sat there answering question after question, I groaned inwardly. *This is exactly why I didn't want to do this. I feel like I'm shopping for a new car instead of looking for a husband.*

Over an hour went by before we finally finished our questionnaires.

"Are you ready?" she asked in a resigned tone.

I closed my eyes and took a deep breath. "Let's do this!"

We hovered our fingers over the Find Matches button.

"On the count of three."

"Oneeee ..."

"Twoooo ..."

"Three!" we said in unison.

We were now official online daters. Let the games begin!

Online Dating

I find it interesting that while online dating is the most direct means of seeking a potential mate, many searching singles are still reluctant to try it. We live in a highly technological society that is perfectly comfortable getting online degrees and doing online shopping. We even have virtual doctor's appointments, so why is Internet dating still such a stumbling block for some? I cannot speak for everyone, but for me, the two main reasons I avoided it were fear and shame.

The first time I mentioned wanting to try online dating, I got an animated lecture from a married friend who was convinced online dating was the fast track to ending up on a missing person's poster. I understood her concerns. I was a little worried myself. However, once I worked up the courage to move past my fears and try it, online dating proved to be much safer than I expected. In fact, it was far safer than some of the dating I had done the traditional way.

The worst thing I experienced doing online dating was unsolicited pictures from a guy that thankfully failed to come through clearly on my phone. Meanwhile, a happenstance meeting with a handsome guy at an ice cream shop involved the police after he began stalking me. Talk about a meet-cute gone wrong!

Seeking safety through limiting your dating options is an illusion. The world is a dangerous place, and dating must be done with caution regardless of the mode of introduction. Use your dating street smarts:

1. Don't give out your address or personal phone number.
2. Don't go to their house alone.
3. Meet in a public place.
4. Consider doing a double-date at first.

If you're still nervous, pack a Taser and ask a friend to follow you in their car and call every few minutes, pretending to be your roommate who just got out of prison.

No, don't do that. Seriously, though, just be careful. Use your street smarts, and whatever you do, don't go out with people you meet at the ice cream parlor ... Those are the real creepers.

In addition to the fear, I also struggled with shame regarding online dating. I mean, how pathetic do you have to be to advertise for a mate online? At least when I went to the singles group, I could pass that off as seeking community. However, with Internet dating, the spouse hunt is blatantly apparent. It can even feel somewhat ... desperate.

Have you felt that?

The secret to overcoming the desperation stigma is to go shopping for a flyswatter. You heard me—go get yourself a flyswatter.

You have two general options for obtaining it: You can get online and order one, or you can go to the store.

If you opt to get it online, you can pick up your phone and have it brought directly to your doorstep—for free—by the end of the day. The whole process will take you about two minutes. Amazon Prime is where it's at, ya'll!

However, if online shopping feels too desperate for you, put the book down, get in the car, head to the nearest store, and wander up and down the aisles until you have a happenstance meet-cute with a flyswatter. I jest, of course, but my illustration makes a good point. Online dating is no more desperate than online shopping. It is merely a platform that facilitates the introductions of available compatible people.

Now that we have addressed the hindrances, let's talk about options. Much like online shopping, there are a plethora of dating sites available. How does one know which to choose? That depends; what are you looking for? Each site or app has a target audience, and with some research, you can determine which one best suits your purposes.

Although starting with one of the free sites may be tempting, I highly discourage that. Not saying you couldn't meet someone of quality on a free site, but as the adage goes, you get what you pay for. Finding a future mate is worth the investment. So pay for a legitimate membership. Most only require an affordable monthly fee.

One of the main benefits of using a paid site is having access to their matching services. Although I was initially put off by the questionnaire, I later found it rather ingenious. Religious beliefs, personal preferences, professional goals, and personality traits are not the fun aspects of a relationship but are crucial areas of compatibility that can determine a relationship's success or failure. I know being matched by an algorithm isn't very romantic, but look at it this way: The algorithm acts as a sort of filter to introduce you to others with similar beliefs, goals, and desires with whom you will have a greater chance of relational success.

Personally, I really enjoyed the fact that the matching technology took a lot of the guesswork out of dating. No more meeting a cute guy, crushing on each other for weeks (or months), someone finally making a move, dating for a month or two, then finding out that his life goal is to be the next Christian rock star while his wife acts as his primary groupie. Not cool, dude, so not cool.

Let's face it, traditional dating does not lend itself to dealing with compatibility aspects at the onset. Going on a first date and getting interviewed against someone's spousal checklist is super awkward. I had a guy do that to me. Totally weirded me out. However, when an algorithm has already asked the awkward questions, you and your date are free to focus on the warm and fuzzies instead of whether or not you both want kids.

Pros and Cons

Regardless of which website one chooses, the pros and cons of online dating are pretty similar.

Pros:	Cons:
1. More Options I met many amazing people whom I never would have known existed otherwise. There was still plenty of fish in the sea. All the good ones were not gone, not even close.	1. More Competition Once, roomie and I realized we were being pursued by the same guy. He was literally copy-pasting his messages. We decided to save him the trouble of choosing, and both said no thanks. Take that, playaa!
2. Less Guesswork The matching services do a lot of the groundwork for you. With so many of the essential things already out in the open, the only thing I had to decide was whether or not there was chemistry.	2. More Miscommunication There were more misunderstandings. Even though we had been "matched," there are crucial things to understanding another person that a computer program cannot capture.

3. More Opportunities The consistent influx of opportunities made the inevitable rejections easier to take. When one person said, "No, thanks," I just moved on to the next message in my inbox.	3. More Rejections Meeting lots of people meant that there were more voices to say "Thanks, but no, thanks."
4. More Efficient Online dating helps people get straight to the point. No more looking, waiting, hoping, praying. See, meet, date, and repeat until you find someone you want to take to the altar.	4. Less Personal People are often more comfortable being rude when they can hide behind a computer. "Ghosting" was more common than in traditional dating.

Overall, I rate my experience with online dating as 8 out of 10. If you have any interest at all, I highly recommend trying it. Like I told the roomie, what have you got to lose? I chose singles groups and online dating options to grow my dating pool. Now it's your turn. What doors do you need to pull open? What intentional avenues for seeking do you need to explore? Regardless of what you try, please don't leave your future up to chance. If a meet-cute comes your way, then by all means, seize the day! Just don't expect it, and for the love of all that is holy, don't sit around and wait for it. Life is what you make it, my friend, so live it intentionally.

CHAPTER TEN

The Ask

"Let me see your online dating matches!" Josi urged me.

"My profile is open on the computer on my desk," I answered.
She darted back to my bedroom.

"You haven't even reached out to half of the people you are matched with!" I could hear her exclaiming from a distance.

"I am waiting for them to initiate," I answered matter-of-factly.

"Why are you doing that?" she retorted.

"It's the man's job to initiate," I volleyed back at her.

"Says who?" Her tone was dumbfounded. "I would never waste my time sitting around waiting for the guys to reach out first. That's dumb."

"Well, then I guess it's a good thing you're not the one sitting around waiting then!" I shot back.

What is it about close friends not being able to mind their own business?

Suddenly, she was quiet.

That's rare of her to give up so easily. I better go check on this.

I walked toward the bedroom, and she met me halfway.

"I messaged all your matches for you," she said as she calmly strolled past.

I stood there in stupefied shock for a moment.

"Yyyy … you did WHAT?!" I stammered.

"Now you don't have to wait anymore," she said with satisfaction.

"What were you thinking?" I fumed. "Now these guys are going to think I'm interested in all of them."

"What were *you* thinking leaving me alone with your profile open?" she answered with a mischievous grin.

Good point. For better or worse, my options were now wide open. I no longer stood on the sidelines, waiting for the guys to initiate. The big ask had gone out, and now the ball was in their court. Now that I stopped to think about it, why was I waiting for them to ask in the first place?

Ladies in Waiting

Imagine with me a culture where women are entirely dependent on men. They cannot enroll in universities, get a job, buy property, get a bank account, have a credit card, apply for a loan, or even initiate a divorce. This oppressive society is not overseas in an underdeveloped country; it is right here, in the history of the United States. These instances of gender discrimination may be unthinkable within the majority of modern, secular society, but a mere fifty years ago, this was the norm. Listen to these testimonies from the women who lived it:

"I wanted to go to college like my brothers, but my dad said it was a waste to educate a woman."

"I applied for a loan and was told that I needed to get my husband or dad to cosign with me because a woman's income was not reliable."

"My husband was ill, so I went to work in the factories, and

I was shamed by my coworkers for taking a job that should have gone to a man."

The above quotes are from real women in my life. This was our culture in America, and it would be still had it not been for the tireless efforts of the women's rights movement. Although gender discrimination has yet to be vanquished entirely, there has been notable progress. Ladies may now pursue an education, enter the career of their choosing, earn an independent wage, buy a house, start a business, and marry the man of their choosing; all because brave men and women fought against the societal restraints that oppressed our grandmothers and great-grandmothers. We have been liberated, ladies! Or have we?

The Modern Mating Dance

You would think that women's rights would have revolutionized the courtship script like it did the rest of society, but it didn't. Instead, the modern mating dance is relatively the same as it was when women were portrayed as happiest at home, vacuuming in their heels.

The hit film *He's Just Not That into You* portrays these stereotypes comically yet poignantly. The main character, Gigi, wants to be a modern woman and take charge of her love life, and yet she still finds herself waiting by the phone for the man to call.

A bartender tries to educate her to take a man at his word and not to read between the lines or look for signs. Gigi doesn't take him at his word and pursues anyway. She ends up being spurned for her aggressiveness and chided by the man she pursued.

> "If a guy wants to date you, *he* will make it happen."—Gigi's love interest.

This sentiment is echoed by others who encourage women to flirt, just not pursue.

"Women asking men on first dates can be taken as aggressive, desperate, and masculine."[28]

Sorry, ladies, society says that you must enter the fray with your hands tied behind your back. You may flutter your eyes and flip your hair, but don't you dare directly express your interest lest the object of your affections spurns you for your "unfeminine" behavior.

Luckily, there are still ladies willing to buck the constraints of society and blaze a new trail. For example, an influencer on Twitter did a social experiment. She challenged her female followers to directly ask out their male crush on a date, just to see what would happen. Interestingly, instead of being horrified at the ladies' "aggressive, desperate, and masculine" behavior, the majority of the men were enthusiastic and even intrigued:

Girl's Text	Guy's Response
Wanna go on a date with me?	Would love to!
Heyyy, wanna go on a date with me?	Heeey, of course!
Will you go to dinner with me next Fri?	Oooh, you taking *me* out? Do you want me to be fancy?

Sounds like the men are pretty happy to be on the receiving end of the pursuit. Why wouldn't they be? Who doesn't like knowing that someone finds them attractive and wants to spend time with them?

Long story short, the courtship script is an unnecessary and unbeneficial societal restraint that hearkens to a culture best left in the history books.

---

[28] https://www.evanmarckatz.com/blog/dating-tips-advice/should-women-ask-men-out-on-first-dates

Your Move

The antiquated courtship script prolongs singleness because it assumes all men are gifted with boldness and prefer to be the pursuer. This is simply not the case.

My friend Sara was gorgeous, godly, outspoken, and hilarious. Although she had no want of interested, bold suitors, she was attracted to quiet, unassuming Sam. She began to send out all the signs she was interested in him: beckoning smiles, lingering after class to talk to him, and inviting him to social gatherings. Sam smiled back, accepted her invitations, and enjoyed their chats.

The chemistry between them was so apparent that our friend circle felt certain Sam would overcome his shyness and ask Sara out. So she waited ... and waited ... for *months*. Sara began to get disillusioned. Why wouldn't Sam pursue her? They were perfect for each other. She grew weary of praying that Sam would pursue her. Instead, she began praying about whether or not to approach him directly and ask if he was interested in her. She sought counsel from a pastor she respected and received a vehement "Absolutely not! I strongly discourage you from doing this. *He* will pursue *you* if he's interested."

Sara submissively went back to waiting, but she couldn't shake the urge to be bold and pursue, so one day she just did it.

"Sam, what do you think about ... us?"

"Us?! Us, how?" he fumbled.

"Us as a couple!" she said with slight exasperation. Had the idea really never even crossed his mind?

"Would that be a positive or a negative thing for you?" he queried breathlessly, barely able to speak for nervousness.

"Positive, of course," she assured with enthusiasm.

That was all it took. Sara and Sam began a relationship then and there, and six months later, Sam proposed. Ironically, the pastor who urged Sara not to pursue Sam performed their wedding ceremony.

At the wedding, I overheard Sam's dad making a fascinating observation.

"I am so glad Sara pursued Sam. He never even had a girlfriend before her because he was too shy to ask anyone out. I was afraid he would be single for life."

What a shame that would have been. I wonder how many other wonderful men are not in relationships because their personalities or experiences cause them to struggle with shyness or insecurity? How many great girls are missing out on these wonderful men because the woman's bold personality is being stifled by the cultural assumption that it is improper for them to initiate?

Waiting on Boaz

Now for the big question: What is the biblical perspective on the traditional courtship script? Society and personal experience aside, what does God have to say on the topic?

Are you familiar with the story of Ruth and Boaz? Popular Christian culture uses their love story to encourage Christian women to learn from Ruth's example and "wait for your Boaz." So how did Ruth become the "wait on the man" poster child? Let's read the story and see.

Quick backstory—Ruth was a Moabite, married to a Jewish man, living in Moab. Her husband died suddenly and left her a penniless widow. Her mother-in-law, Naomi, is also a widow, and after the death of her sons, she decides to leave Moab and return to her homeland, Israel.

In an act of selfless love, Ruth leaves her people, the Moabites, and accompanies Naomi, knowing this choice will most likely mean she will never remarry and, thus, lead a life of desperate poverty.

However, a serendipitous turn of events unfolds once they reach Israel. They arrive at the beginning of the harvest, and Ruth goes to glean (gather grain behind the harvesters).

Gleaning was ancient Israel's welfare system. The Levitical law provided for the poor by allowing them to take part in the harvest of the landowners by gathering the grain that naturally fell during the reaping. This is where things began to get interesting.

> She happened to be in the portion of the field belonging to Boaz, who was from Elimelech's family (*Ruth 2:3*).

Elimelech is Naomi's late husband. The mention of Boaz as a member of Naomi's husband's family is intentional and essential. If a man died without a son, the Levitical laws stated that someone from his family was to step up as "a kinsman-redeemer" and marry his widow to provide her with a family, provision, and protection. Boaz is described as a man of noble character and prominent in the community, and he notices Ruth.

> Boaz asked his servant who was in charge of the harvesters, "Whose young woman is this?" The servant answered, "She is the young Moabite woman who returned with Naomi from the territory of Moab ... Then Boaz said to Ruth, "Listen, my daughter. Don't go and gather grain in another field, and don't leave this one, but stay here close to my female servants. See which field they are harvesting, and follow them. Haven't I ordered the young men not to touch you? When you are thirsty, go and drink from the jars the young men have filled" (*Ruth 2:5–9*).

After his little speech, Boaz continues to shamelessly pile attention on Ruth for the rest of the day. He invites her to sit with him at lunch and even tells his reapers to drop handfuls of grain for her on purpose. If I didn't know any better, I would say he was exhibiting all the nonverbal signs of being positively smitten.

When Ruth returns home with twice as much grain as was expected, a surprised Naomi asks her where on earth she got it all. When Ruth mentions Boaz, Naomi immediately recognizes the importance of this "chance" meeting. She informed Ruth that Boaz was one of their eligible family redeemers and instructed her to only glean in Boaz's fields for the remainder of the harvest.

Now for the happy ending—Ruth remains with Boaz's reapers for the duration of the harvest, allowing him to observe what a faithful, godly woman she is. During the end-of-season celebration, Boaz invites Ruth as his companion, praises her for faithfully waiting for him to initiate, and asks her to be his wife as his friends and family cheer. Ruth's patience earned her a good man, and they all lived happily ever after.

Great ending, right? There's just one problem—that's not what happened.

The mantra "waiting for my Boaz" might look good on a T-shirt and make for a great hashtag, but in reality, Ruth did anything *but* "wait for her Boaz."

Here's what really happened: Ruth heeded Naomi's advice and spent the harvest season faithfully gleaning but receiving no offers of relationship or marriage from Boaz. Luckily, her mother-in-law had a few more tricks up her sleeve. Naomi informs Ruth about the laws that provide her with a family redeemer. According to the law, Ruth's admirer, Boaz, is eligible to marry and provide for her. Boaz will be having a party that night, and Naomi tells Ruth to dress up nice and propose to Boaz ... in secret.

Wait, what?! Yeah, that's right. Ruth didn't wait. She needs a husband, and Boaz is on a short list of potential suitors, so she takes matters into her own hands. She makes herself as attractive and alluring as possible. Then she goes in for the kill. She sneaks onto the threshing floor at night and waits 'til Boaz has "well drunk." Then she uncovers his tootsies so he'll get cold and wake so she can pop the question.

Talk about boldness! Instead of chiding her directness, Boaz praises her.

> May the Lord bless you, my daughter. You have shown more *kindness* now than before because you have not pursued younger men, whether rich or poor. Now don't be afraid, my daughter. I will do for you whatever you say since all the people in my town know that you are a woman of *noble* character (*Ruth 3:10–11*; emphasis added).

Ladies, society and popular Christian culture label bold women as aggressive and unfeminine, but the Bible deems them as kind and noble. There is no need to sit around waiting on the men. Do you have the strength of boldness? Use it to snag a good man. Chances are, if you are bold, you are attracted to people whose strengths are different from yours. If boldness is not your man's strength, that's OK. Help a guy out and let your strengths make up for his weaknesses so his strengths can make up for your weaknesses. Take a lesson from Ruth. Stop waiting for your Boaz. Go get him!

CHAPTER ELEVEN

A Real Man

Mitch, like many men, was taught that to be worthy of a woman's love and affection, he had to have his life entirely in order. At the very least, he should have his education taken care of so he had a chance of being able to reasonably support a family.

He first heard this message as a young teenager. When he mentioned that he was interested in dating, his parents immediately shut the idea down.

"You are not mature enough to have a girlfriend. You need to finish high school and college first. No girl is going to want to date a guy who can't take care of her."

He put off dating and did his due diligence.

- High school diploma: Check
- College: Check

To his surprise, businesses were not falling all over his hard-won degree as he thought they would. A degree was only the beginning; now he needed experience. He finally found an entry-level position and began bringing in a steady paycheck.

I've got it together enough to date now, he thought. Sadly, the ladies disagreed.

"You work where?"

"You're only a junior employee?"

"You expect your wife to work too?"

Mitch reasoned that he must not have arrived yet, so he worked harder and moved up. More money should mean more honeys, right? Nope.

"You're the perfect guy, except for ..."

"If only we had met sooner or later."

He was more than discouraged. "What were girls looking for? Perfection?"

He reached out to a spiritual mentor for some comfort and direction.

"Sounds like you've been pursuing the wrong girls. You should only pursue a woman if you know she could be the one. You don't want to lead anyone on. Pray and ask God to lead you."

So the next time he saw a cute girl at church, instead of asking her out, he prayed. In an effort to guard his heart and hers, he tried to get to know her from a distance. Can't pursue unless you expect to say "I do." There was just one problem—how can you know if you do or don't if you aren't in a relationship?

This is too much pressure. I'm ready to just forget the whole thing, he thought in exasperation.

His Image, His Glory

It is too much pressure. The religious and societal demands that a man has it all together in every way to be counted a real man is unfair, unrealistic, and most of all, untrue. So let's silence cultural expectations for a moment and see what God has to say about being a man.

Contrary to society, which says a man is defined by what he does, God defines a man based on what he is, the image and glory of God.

> Then God said, Let us make man in our image, according to our likeness. So God created man in his own image (*Genesis 1:26–27*).

> A man should not cover his head, because he is the image and glory of God … (*1 Corinthians 11:7*).

While both men and women are said to be made in the image of God, the man, in particular, is referred to as the glory of God. The Greek word for glory used in this verse is *Doxa*. According to the NAS New Testament Greek Lexicon, this glory is understood as the magnificence, excellence, preeminence, dignity, and grace of God Himself. Gentlemen, God has given you an innate worth described in the most glorious of terms. What you have to offer a woman does not come primarily from what you have accomplished or can provide. It comes from who you are.

That being said, it is essential to remember that while the demand that a man have it *all* together *all* the time is unrealistic, it is equally unrealistic to expect a woman to gleefully hitch her life to yours if all you have to offer her is a train wreck. You don't need to have "arrived," per se, but make sure your train is at least on the tracks.

If you've made decisions that have left your life messy, that's OK. Clean it up and choose better this time! Mistakes are part of being human. Failure is an event, not an identity. Rise, man of God, and get that train back on track!

Man of God

The glory of the Lord dwells within a man innately. However, a man's decision whether or not to reflect that glory will naturally affect his desirability. To attract a godly woman, you must choose to be a man of God.

The Bible is full of scriptures describing what it looks like to truly reflect the glory of God within you, man of God.

> But you, man of God, flee from these things, and pursue righteousness, godliness, faith, love, endurance, and gentleness. Fight the good fight of the faith (*1 Timothy 6:11–12*).

> He has told you, O man, what is good; and what does the LORD require of you but to do justice, and to love kindness, and to walk humbly with your God? (*Micah 6:8 ESV*)

A man of God is primarily concerned with doing justice, developing godly character, and fighting the good fight of faith. This is how God is most glorified and what a worthy wife will be most attracted to. However, I must warn you that being a man of God is risky business. You will encounter resistance from the world, your flesh, and the devil himself, who wants nothing more than to spiritually castrate you and hide all traces of God's glory within you. You will be beaten down, suffer ridicule, and have to *fight* the good fight of faith. However, you can do it because of who you are. When you get discouraged, take inspiration from this speech in one of America's favorite underdog stories.

> Let me tell you something you already know. The world ain't all sunshine and rainbows. It's a very mean and nasty place, and I don't care how tough

you are, it will beat you to your knees and keep you there permanently if you let it. You, me, or nobody is gonna hit as hard as life. But it ain't about how hard ya hit. It's about how hard you can get hit and keep moving forward. How much you can take and keep moving forward. That's how winning is done! Now, if you know what you're worth, then go out and get what you're worth!
—Rocky Balboa

Although the character Rocky Balboa is fictional, the man who created him knew something about getting back up when life knocks you down. Sylvester Stallone was a struggling young actor living in slums, with nothing to his name but a dream and a dog. After a while, he was down to just a dream, having sold his beloved dog because he couldn't afford to feed it. Then the genuinely starving artist attended a boxing match one evening and was so inspired that he went home and wrote the script for the first *Rocky* movie in three days. A studio was impressed with the story and offered to buy it, hoping to cast a well-known actor in the lead role. However, Stallone insisted that he be cast in the role of Rocky. Although the studio offered him an enormous amount of money, Stallone was immovable. No Sly, no buy. Eventually, the studio relented and gave him the role.

Rocky was a knockout success, receiving nine Oscar nominations and three wins, including Best Picture. The character Rocky Balboa became one of America's most inspirational underdogs, and Stallone became an icon, a symbol of grit and persistence.

Has life knocked you down, man of God? Get back up. Are you tired and frustrated? Learn to rest instead of quit. Is the going slow and arduous? Keep moving forward one step at a time. Don't give up because you have a quest to complete.

The Quest for a Wife

Aside from the ask-seek-knock prayer formula we have already discussed, the Bible does not have a step-by-step guide for obtaining a wife. However, there are some biblical principles that can help guide you on this worthy quest.

> A house and wealth are inherited from fathers, but a prudent wife is from the LORD (*Proverbs 19:14*).

Your mama and daddy might leave you money, but "money can't buy you love." Only the Lord can provide a wife. Does that mean that all a man has to do is wait to be gifted with one? No! As a man of God, you are called to action, not complacency.

> A man who finds a wife finds a good thing and obtains favor from the Lord (*Proverbs 18:22*).

It does not say he who is *given* a wife or he who *stumbles* upon a wife. It says he who *finds* a wife. Common sense tells us that the one doing the finding is the one doing the seeking.

While the Bible does not have a guide regarding how to find a wife, it does offer a rather detailed guide concerning what kind of girl to be searching for. Are you familiar with Proverbs 31? You might not be considering PCC teaches it almost exclusively to women. In truth, it was not originally intended for a female audience. Proverbs 31 is the words of a mother to her son, telling him what he should be looking for in a wife of quality. Such a wife is wise, caring, industrious, loyal, and capable—a true treasure. Treasure is not something to be found lying around. Treasure is usually hidden and must be searched for diligently. A quality wife is no different. If you want to find a wife like the mother describes, then be prepared to search hard.

> Who can find a wife of quality? She is far more
> precious than jewels (*Proverbs 31:10*).

Are you ready to begin your quest? Then rise, man of God. Just because you do not have everything together does not disqualify you from pursuing a godly wife. Life is a journey. Spiritual maturity is a process. As long as you are regularly striving to honor God and live according to His Word, you can offer the women of this day something rare and priceless. Do you want an excellent wife? I've got good news—she wants you too! Now go put in the hard work to find her.

CHAPTER TWELVE

The One?

I am an avid fan of the *Once Upon a Time* series. Seriously, what could be better than having all your favorite fairy-tale characters become part of the real world?

Once is set in a sleepy little town called Storybrooke. While it may seem quaint, Storybrooke is actually a prison. All the fairy-tale heroes are trapped there in an alternate reality because of the Evil Queen's curse. The curse was created with the express purpose of derailing all the fairy-tale romances. Prince Charming and Snow White don't recognize each other. Beauty and the Beast are separated by prison bars. Cinderella is back in her rags and doesn't even believe in love.

Interestingly, despite their amnesia, everyone is still inexplicably drawn to their soulmate. That's the power of true love, my friend. In fact, as the story unfolds, we learn that true love's kiss is the only thing that can break the curse, reunite the lovers, and restore everyone's true identity. I know it's cheesy, but we all have our guilty pleasures.

People relish a good love story, and the quest for "true love" is at the heart of them all. True love is what we are all searching for. I dare say it is why you are reading this book. But how does one find true love? What is the secret? According to Hallmark, Disney, and Hollywood, true love is found in the arms of your soulmate, your other half, the "one" meant for you. I'd like to tell you that this concept has some merit beyond the silver screen, but unfortunately, the origin of a "right one" for everyone is just as fictional as the tales in *Once Upon a Time*.

The idea can be traced back to the Greek philosopher Plato. In Plato's *Symposium* on love, he describes a fictional philosophical conversation concerning the origins of love. The character Aristophanes explains love through a heartfelt tale of humans having originally existed as one being made from two entities. These dual beings were mighty, and to thwart a takeover, the god Zeus separated the humans into two halves. After being torn asunder, the humans were so consumed with finding their *other half* that they no longer posed a threat. According to Aristophanes, this is why humans long to love and be loved in return.

> This, then, is the source of our desire to love each other. Love is born into every human being; it calls back the halves of our original nature together; it tries to make one out of two and heal the wound of human nature. Each of us, then, is a "matching half" of a human whole ... and each of us is always seeking the half that matches him.—Plato's *Symposium*[29]

This Greek idea of a specific "one" for everyone spread across the western world until it came to Great Britain. There it was repackaged by the poet Samuel Taylor Coleridge, who coined the term *soul-mate*.

---

[29] https://www.laphamsquarterly.org/eros/platos-other-half

"To be happy in marriage life … one must have
a soul-mate."[30]

The idea of a soulmate continued to grow and became firmly
rooted at the heart of American culture's romance narrative. An
example of this is the smash hit movie *The Notebook*. This story
is arguably one of the most popular soulmate tales of modern
times. Two teenagers, Allie and Noah, meet and fall in love in a
whirlwind summer romance. Though they are parted, no amount
of time or other loves can make them forget each other. They were
simply meant to be. Who can forget the aging Noah's declaration
of true love?

> I am nothing special. But in one respect, I have
> succeeded as gloriously as anyone who's ever lived:
> I've loved another with all my heart and soul; and
> to me, this has always been enough.
> —Duke (Noah)

Oh, to love and be loved like *that*. Such love requires a true
meeting of hearts and souls and, according to the notion of
soulmates, can only exist between two people made for each
other.

This secular idea of a soulmate eventually infiltrated popular
Christian culture, where it was Christianized into "the one" God
has for you. This message resonates within Christian life in a
variety of ways. For example, Christian singles are encouraged to
pray for the Lord to lead them to the "right one" with example
prayers such as this one: "If it is Your will, guide them, Lord, to
the partner You have chosen for them. Give them the wisdom and
direct them in their pursuit to choose the right person."[31]

---

[30] Coleridge, Samuel T. *Marriage: A Letter to a Young Lady*, 1822.
[31] https://christianstt.com/prayer-marriage-god-chosen-life-partner/

Christian guides to help one discern if they have met the right one abound:

- 6 Ways to Tell If He's the One You've Been Praying For[32]
- 10 Steps to Meet the One God Has for You[33]

Happily married Christian couples attribute their success to finding the "right one."

Unhappily married couples are told their woes are brought about by them having chosen the "wrong one."

Finding, verifying, and choosing God's choice for you is paramount within popular Christian culture's message to singles. However, it is rooted in Greek philosophy and secular fantasy, not the Bible.

In addition to being unbiblical, it is also impractical. The belief in only *one* right person for everyone means that *one* mistake would send everyone's love life into chaos.

Imagine the implication if the "right one" for Susie is Tommy, but Susie mistakenly marries Benny. Now that Susie is no longer available, Tommy decides to settle for Penny. That means Penny has left Billy, the "right one" for her, in the lurch. He then settles for someone else, and the cycle repeats itself ad nauseam.

The domino effect of having only one right one for everyone would be endless. Eventually, there would be nothing but mismatched couples all outside of God's will for their relationships.

Analysis Paralysis

Sadly, the quest for the "right one" can be the very thing that keeps you from finding a mate. To avoid choosing the wrong one,

---

[32] https://theprayingwoman.com/6-ways-to-tell-if-hes-the-one-youve-been-praying-for/

[33] https://agwuniversity.teachable.com/p/total-access

many singles become trapped in analysis paralysis. They don't want to decide wrong, so they don't decide at all. Instead, they defer to God and ask Him to lead them to *His* choice for them. Unfortunately, God is not running a Dear Abby column. He is not obligated to dish out divine revelation every time people come to a crossroads in life. I learned this the hard way.

I had received God's call to enter the ministry vocationally, and now it was time to choose which seminary to attend. Convinced that this decision held eternal weight, I researched schools to determine which one would be the best option and prayed diligently for God to show me the right choice. I narrowed down the possibilities until I arrived at my top three. I applied to all three and prayed that God would give me favor with the one he had chosen for me. Unfortunately, all of them accepted me. Now I had a decision to make. I didn't feel qualified to decide, so I tried to pawn my responsibility onto God.

"God, where do you want me to go?" I prayed with expectant fervor. "Please lead me to the seminary you have already chosen for me."

I didn't expect a vocal answer or the school's name to be written across the sky. I just wanted God to "whisper to my spirit" or something like that so I would have the assurance that I was making the right choice. Do you know what God said? Nothing, that's what. Heaven was silent. The harder I prayed, the quieter it got. Finally, God's silence and my dependence reached a stalemate, and I began a cycle of analysis paralysis. To not choose poorly, I was choosing nothing. I shared my dilemma with my ministry mentor. His response startled me.

"Harmony, it's not like you're trying to choose between going to seminary or becoming a stripper! All these schools are great choices. Just pick one!" he urged me in exasperation.

Just pick one? Could it really be that simple? Yes, it was. God had provided me with several good options, and it was my responsibility to choose among them.

The same is true when it comes to choosing a mate. God provides the options, but the choice is up to you, my friend. Gary Thomas, the author of *Sacred Search*, makes this powerful observation:

> There is nothing in scripture that suggests there is just one person we're "supposed" to marry. Proverbs 31 urges young men to be guided by a woman's faith and character in making their choice—there is no mention of second-guessing some divine destiny.[34]

God provides guidance and direction regarding whom to marry, but He will not decide for us. The relationship between God's sovereignty and human responsibility is a both/and, not an either/or. The Lord does not choose for us without our consent, nor do we choose for ourselves without His direction. The Lord provides the parameters, and you choose from within His parameters.

Divine Guidance Methods

In his book *Knowing the Will of God*, Bruce Waltke lists six biblical methods for discerning the will of God. In this section, I apply these methods to discerning God's leading in the search for a spouse.

I

The primary method of divine guidance is the Bible. If you want to know what the Lord thinks/wants, then read His Word. Attempting to understand the mind of God without knowing His

---

[34] https://garythomas.com/2015/01/05/goddidnttellyoumarryyourspouse/

Word is like taking an exam without first taking the class. If you can discipline yourself to read and apply God's Word regularly, you will find that you already know what God wants without relying on a personal word from God. Divine revelation is not needed concerning subjects the Lord has already clearly addressed in His Word.

Right after graduating college, I met a dashing young soldier while on a work trip in San Francisco. He sparked up a conversation with me while standing in line at the Pier Nine Ghirardelli chocolate shop and asked me to sit with him. We had a wonderful conversation over our treat that was finished far too soon. We said our farewells, and I walked back to the trolley stop with my coworkers. Just as the trolley was pulling up, Don Juan, as my colleagues dubbed him, came rushing down the hill and handed me his phone number.

"I want to see you again, Harmony. Please come back to San Francisco someday."

The trolley pulled up, and I stood in the back, gazing at him until he was out of view. It was just like being in a movie. There was only one problem: During our first phone conversation, I discovered he was not a Christian. I knew about the biblical mandate that Christians only marry other believers, but surely a friendship couldn't hurt. After all, I might be able to lead him to Jesus. He assured me that he would never object to me practicing Christianity, but he did not feel ready to commit to following Jesus yet. Nevertheless, I felt sure that my influence would be what he needed to come to Jesus. So I began to pray diligently to that end and also ask God if I should finally give in and call our friendship what it was—a dating relationship.

Heaven was silent again because I already knew the answer. I did not need a special word from God on the matter. God had already made His thoughts on marriage between believers and unbelievers clear in His Word. By ignoring God's written Word, I was living in disobedience, and no amount of pretending to seek

God's direction on the matter would justify it. The relationship self-combusted after a few short months, and I was left with needless wounds that could have been avoided.

Missionary dating is a recipe for disaster, my friend. Take God at His Word, apply what He has already said in scripture and you will save yourself a world of heartache.

II

The second means of divine guidance is through the desires of our hearts. A regular intake of the Bible shapes our minds and hearts to reflect the heart and mind of God. As God's Word renews our minds, our desires begin to reflect His desires (Psalm 37:4, Philippians 2:13). Righteous desires that line up with God's Word and flow from a heart devoted to the Lord can be another tool used to guide believers.

Lance was introduced to Kerrie through his parents. He was new to town, so his mom asked her best friend to have her daughter recommend some good churches in the area. Lance began attending church with Kerrie and found himself attracted to her. Who wouldn't be? Kerrie is smart, beautiful, and loves the Lord. Should Lance begin praying that God would show him if He should ask Kerrie out? No.

Lance has already received adequate direction to decide on his own. Kerrie is within the biblical guidelines for a spouse, and Lance desires to date her. He can proceed confidently. On the flip side, if Lance did not feel any desire to date Kerrie, he should heed that lack of desire as a sign that he should pursue someone else.

III

The third method of guidance comes through the wise counsel of others. Once you have considered God's Word and your desires, you can also seek wise counsel from others (Proverbs

1:5). Sometimes an outside perspective can do wonders to help us see things more clearly. Just ensure the counsel you receive is from someone who has demonstrated godly character and made decisions you wish to emulate.

Had I heeded wise counsel, I could have avoided the heartbreak I experienced with Ricky Although he was a believer and I had a strong desire to date him, two older women in my life warned me against it. Their years on this earth and their outside perspective were able to see things that I could not. Make use of the wise counsel that God has provided from within your circle of trusted fellow believers.

IV

The fourth method is when God guides through providence. Paul refers to God's will being recognized through a circumstance in Romans 1:10.

> Always asking in my prayers that if it is somehow in God's will, I may now at last succeed in coming to you (*Romans 1:10*).

God is sovereign over all things, even the minutest details of our lives. Circumstances are never a coincidence. That's why when things just inexplicably fall into place, people refer to it as a "God thing."

With this in mind, have circumstances brought you a person who meets the previous four guidelines? Then you can consider them a strong candidate. On the contrary, have circumstances prevented you from connecting with someone despite your best efforts? If the circumstances do not change, it may be God guiding you elsewhere.

V

The fifth way God guides us is through our good sense. God has created us with intelligent minds. We are capable of thinking through issues and coming to reasonable, sound decisions that are within the revealed will of God.

"You may do whatever seems best to you ...
according to the will of your God (*Ezra 7:18*).

If you want to know if the person you are dating is a good fit for you, then use your head.

While in seminary, I went on a few consecutive dates with a handsome preacher boy. Our time together had been going well, and he asked me to go steady on Valentine's Day. Well played, I must say. He was attractive, a strong Christian, and had other admirable qualities I really liked. However, he planned to pursue a career in Christian music and tour, while I desired to settle down and do student ministry in the local church. He made it clear that he would want his wife to tour with him, and I knew I didn't want that life. I decided to stop dating based on my assessment that our life goals were incompatible.

Do you have someone who you think would make a great spouse for you based on your common sense? Then move forward. However, if you have feelings for someone but know that the two of you are not a good fit, then move on. Listen to your head and not just your heart. I assure you the old adage "Love is enough" is not true.

VI

The final and least common way that the Lord leads is through divine revelation. There are a few instances in scripture where God did, indeed, specifically tell someone whom to marry.

We will look at them together and determine what we can apply from them.

The first example is in the case of Hosea and Gomer. God directed Hosea to marry a woman known for promiscuity and remain with her despite her infidelity. His marriage was to illustrate God's faithfulness to Israel despite their idolatry. As you can imagine, Hosea's marriage was one of great heartbreak.

The second example is in the case of Mary and Joseph. As you may know, Mary became pregnant with Jesus before she and Joseph were married. Joseph was less than convinced that the pregnancy was brought about by the Holy Spirit. Joseph knew that if he made what appeared to be infidelity public, Mary's life would be in danger.

As Joseph contemplated what to do, God used divine revelation to tell Joseph that the baby was, indeed, divinely conceived and directed him to wed Mary. Joseph's choice to marry her despite her apparent premarital pregnancy would make it appear that he was the father and had been party to her supposed sin. This would have brought disgrace upon him. God's choice of a spouse for Joseph would require him to sacrifice his good name.

God did not give Hosea and Joseph a direct word regarding who to marry to make their romantic dreams come true and spare them relational trouble. Instead, He gave them a direct word because God's choice of a spouse for them would require them to go against Mosaic law, their desires, and even common sense.

God used divine revelation not to make their relational dreams come true, but to communicate to these men to ignore the usual methods of guidance and enter into marriages that would cause them suffering to fulfill God's greater purpose. Still interested in enlisting God as your personal matchmaker?

Should you be one of the very few to receive a special word from God concerning whom to marry, heed it. Just don't expect it. Divine revelation is rare and usually occurs during out-of-the-ordinary circumstances when no other method of guidance will do. It is not a regular occurrence God uses to guide Christians in everyday life decisions.

There is no need to over-spiritualize the process of seeking a spouse. If you apply the first five methods of divine guidance to your love life, you will be more than prepared to choose wisely for yourself. God may have sent Gabriel to direct Mary and Joseph's love life, but don't expect that for your own. You are not destined to parent the Savior of the world. Gabriel has better things to do than run around guiding indecisive Christians in matters of love. If you absolutely must have angelic direction, I suggest you consult Cupid. Love is his department.

True Soulmates

True soulmates are not found; they are chosen. We get to choose the one we allow to know us most intimately, the one we will share the joys and trials of life with. As a couple continues to choose each other to build a life with, to grow old with, to laugh and cry with, one day they wake up and realize that their souls are forever knit together, not because they were made for each other, but because of the love that grew from continually choosing each other. The task before you is not to find "the one," my friend. Your task is to choose "the one."

PART 4

PERSONAL OBSTACLES

Attitudes and Behaviors that Prolong Singleness

CHAPTER THIRTEEN

Settling for Real

You come to love, not by finding the perfect person,
but by seeing an imperfect person perfectly.
—Sam Keen

I paced the room nervously, frequently glancing at my phone. Any minute now, I would get a phone call from my most promising online dating match. Up until now, we had only communicated via e-mail. Now it was time to talk for real.

Ring! Ring!

I reached for the phone then hesitated.

What if he has a weird voice or annoying accent? I thought.

Ring! Ring!

I better answer before he gives up. Oh please, God, don't let him have an awful voice.

"Hello?" I said in the sweetest Southern drawl I could muster.

"Hello, Harmony." The words glided smoothly over my ears like warm syrup on a pancake.

Pleasant voice: Check.

What followed was the best conversation I had ever had with a man. Mr. Match was so pleasant to talk to. I was so excited.

Maybe there was hope! Then he dropped this bombshell: "So great to know there are still wonderful Christian girls like you out there. I'm hoping to find someone I can trust to be faithful. My ex and I divorced this year ..."

I heard nothing else after that. I finally met a guy I'm interested in, and he had to be recently divorced, probably on the rebound, and in need of some serious healing time. I just couldn't catch a break. I determined to hide my disappointment and bring the conversation to a close as painlessly as possible.

"I am so sorry to hear about that," I said with as much positivity as I could muster. "I will be praying for you. I don't think it is appropriate for us to start seeing each other so soon after your divorce. You need time to process and heal. I tell you what, if you're still available in a year (*Lord knows I'll still be single at this rate*), then give me a call, and we can try again."

I don't know why I arbitrarily picked one year. It just sounded adequate. To my surprise, He was not the least bit put off.

"So great talking to you, Harmony. I wish you all the best from life. So I can call you back on this day next year?"

Oh, why does he have to be so romantic? My resolve is weakening.

"Yes, if you're still interested. Call me back then," I said hurriedly before I changed my mind.

We hung up, and I crawled into bed, the most dejected I had been in a long time.

All the next day, I could think of nothing but Mr. Match. I decided to call Josi. She always knew how to help me sort things out.

"You asked him to wait a whole year!" she practically shrieked.

"He needs time to heal before he enters another relationship," I argued. *At least that's what all those relationship books say.* "He probably has all sorts of baggage, probably on the rebound. I don't want to settle. I'm waiting for God's best."

"It's not your place to say how much time he needs to heal or to decide where he is emotionally," she countered as she launched into one of her monologues. "For me, choosing to move on would be part of the healing instead of just wallowing alone. You really like him. Now you're going to refuse a relationship with him just because something in his past is not ideal? Why would you do that?"

Standards

Her question caught me off guard and caused me to reevaluate my stance. Mr. Match met the biblical standards for a potential mate; he just didn't meet my personal standards. I didn't want a divorcee at all. I wanted someone who had been faithfully saving his heart and body for just me.

However, my time in the elder singles club had shown me that "never marrieds" were harder and harder to come by. Still, if I had to *settle* for being a second wife, I at least wanted my husband to have been divorced for an adequate amount of time to have gotten over the first one. What was an adequate amount of time though? A year sounded perfectly reasonable until I talked to Josi. Was her way better? Who got to decide that?

Eventually, I acknowledged that I rejected Mr. Match because I was already in love with someone else. Mr. Perfect had stolen my heart years ago. He was ideal. He was sold out for Jesus. His character was impeccable. He had the best personality. We had the same interests and goals. Indeed, he was perfect. Which begs the question, if he was so perfect, then why didn't I just date him? Unfortunately, Mr. Perfect had one glaring flaw—he wasn't real.

Mr. Perfect was the ideal mate I had been imagining, hoping, and praying for, but he only existed in my imagination. I had been looking for someone like him for years, but no one could ever quite measure up. I was in love, not with a person but with an ideal—an ideal mate that would lead to the ideal life I had envisioned.

Before you think I'm out of my mind, take a moment and

imagine yourself married. See that person beside you in your mind's eye? What are they like? Chances are you are picturing someone whose appearance, personality, interests, strengths, and background are exactly to your liking; your ideal mate, in other words. Depending on your personality, your ideal mate may present themselves in the form of preferences and expectations for whom you will marry; your ideal spouse qualifications, if you will. As the CEO of your affections, you use this ideal to categorize potential mates. Those who meet your predetermined preferences and expectations go into your "hopefuls" category, while those who don't are exiled to the dreaded "friends zone."

"So what if I have standards?" you may ask. "Of course, I know that no one's truly perfect, but I have the right to look for what I want in a mate."

Of course, you do. We all have the right to hold out for our ideal mates. However, we do not have the right to demand our ideal from God. People often wail that God has denied them the gift of marriage. In truth, they have denied themselves marriage because they refuse to "settle" for anyone less than their ideal mate. While we are on this topic, rid your mind of the concept of settling in terms of dating. The only people you will ever date are custom-designed image-bearers of Almighty God. He considers every one of them worth dying for. You cannot settle for someone of such immense worth.

That being said, we all come with our own hang-ups and character flaws. The only people who will ever enter into marriage are two sinners. Your job is not to evaluate whether or not someone is *worthy* of you. Your job is to evaluate whether or not you and your person of interest are a good fit for each other. This process will involve considering your standards and preferences, but beware of dating with what Ben Stuart calls "a consumer instead of companion mentality."[35] God is not a

---

[35] https://www.youtube.com/watch?v=F4da5mTLlTQ

coffee shop barista. You cannot walk into the dating pool, layout your list of spousal preferences, and expect Him to produce a customized hottie latte for you. God creates people to *His* liking, not *ours*.

Preferences

Mitch and Misty were out on their first date since the birth of their first child.

"Man, it feels good to be just the two of us again," Mitch said as he sank into the seat and heaved a sigh of relief. "You look beautiful tonight, sweet—"

"What up, guys!" Andy bellowed as he appeared out of nowhere and eagerly slid into the booth beside Misty. "I haven't seen ya'll in forever," Andy continued as he helped himself to their appetizer.

"Hey, Andy, it's our first time out *just the two of us* since the baby," Mitch said, hoping Andy would get the hint.

"No kidding!" Andy went on obliviously as he signaled the waiter to bring him a beverage. "Can't wait to catch up with you guys. How's parenthood?"

Mitch smiled apologetically at Misty and gave in to the inevitable. After they got home that evening, Mitch gave voice to his aggravation.

"Andy clearly has too much time on his hands. We have got to get that guy a wife!"

Mitch and Misty had tried to set Andy up a few times, but he was still "waiting on the Lord." He may have been content to keep waiting, but the young parents were desperate to get some privacy. So the next day they borrowed a few pictures from Andy's social media and posted an ad: *Christian Bachelor Seeks Wife: Could You Be the One?*

It was meant to be a joke within their friend group, but the next thing they knew, girls from all over the country started sending in applications:

- Cassidy from the Midwest wants a date.
- Emily from the mountains is interested.
- Laura from the South wants to put in an application.

The community waited in suspense as Andy reviewed the candidates. Who would the Christian Bachelor choose?

- Candidate A? Too young.
- Candidate B? Too old.
- Candidate C? Too blonde.
- Candidate D? Too brunette.

Would you believe that he turned all the girls down?
Every ... single ... one.
When Mitch asked him why, Andy shrugged and said, "None of them have everything I am looking for."
Mitch threw up his hands in exasperation. "Dude, you're not looking for a wife. You're looking for a unicorn."

Expectations

A friend of mine once shared a poignant story from her youth regarding spousal expectations. She adored her dad. He was proof good men still existed. She felt if she held out long enough, she would find someone like him.

"Why aren't you staying with any of the guys you've been dating?" her dad asked one day.

"All these guys are just so immature!" she said with an exasperated sigh. "I want a mature man with rock-solid character who knows how to love and care for me like you do for Mom.

None of the guys I know are like that. Why can't I find a guy like you?"

"Honey! I'm sixty-five years old. Do you want to marry a sixty-five-year-old? It took years for me to get where I am today. You would have hated me when I was your age, and sometimes your Mom did!"

"After that, I realized my expectations were unrealistic," my friend admitted. "I had been clinging to the fantasy of basically finding the spiritual maturity of Jesus within a twenty-something-year-old movie-star body. That wasn't going to happen."

Expectations are acceptable as long as they are reasonable. Take a moment, write your expectations out, and then ask yourself if anyone in your dating pool, including yourself, measures up to your list. If not, it might be time to consider whether or not your expectations are unrealistic.

Standards are good. Expectations are unavoidable. Preferences are natural. However, holding out for someone who meets *all* your ideals will lead to prolonged singleness because ideal mates are not real. I am going to say that again—THEY ARE NOT REAL! You cannot marry them. You cannot hold their hand. You cannot build a life with them. You cannot start a family with them. You can only do these things with real people.

The actual people you have to choose from as potential mates may have some or even many of your preferences, but they won't have them all. Also, they will come with faults, weaknesses, and things about them that are the opposite of your ideal. Faults are unavoidable. Acknowledge that and decide which ones you are willing to deal with.

After my conversation with Josi, I did some serious soul-searching. I eventually acknowledged that I was not coming without baggage either. In the end, I decided that as a flawed individual myself, I should give him a chance. I texted Mr. Match again.

Harmony: "I feel I was too hasty in insisting you wait a year to contact me. It is not my place to dictate how much time you need to heal and process what you've been through. I ask that you take time to work through this hurt with God, and when you feel like you're ready to move on, I would love to hear from you again."

Mr. Match: "So excited to hear from you again, Harmony. I will do as you say. I look forward to talking to you again in the future."

Regardless of whether or not it would work out with Mr. Match, I knew I had made a big step toward escaping unwanted singleness.

Instead of obsessing about finding my ideal, I began to notice all the real people around me and appreciate them for who God had made them. I no longer hastily assigned people who didn't meet my criteria to the friend zone.

Letting go of my ideal mate opened a world of possibilities for me, and it can work for you too. Stop clinging to your ideal mate and give some of your fellow real people a chance. You just might be surprised.

CHAPTER FOURTEEN

Your Best Self

You know that breakup line, "It's not you, it's me"? Spoiler alert: It's usually a lie. No one breaks up with someone they're really into because they can't handle their significant other's awesomeness. In truth, they are just not interested. That's OK. Rejection is a natural part of dating. No one can be everybody's Chick-Fil-A sauce. However, when one is getting a lack of interest the majority of the time, it might mean that there is more to the story. Sometimes the reasons behind prolonged singleness are not caused by bad theology or cultural hindrances. Sometimes they are caused by people not showing up as their best selves.

Remember Andy from the social media Christian Bachelor? Well, he finally got reasonable with his expectations and decided to give dating a shot again. He started an online dating profile and waited for the applicants to come rolling in. Unfortunately, the ladies he was pursuing were not as eager to move forward as he was.

> Girl 1: "Can't today."
> Girl 2: "Not ready for a relationship"
> Girl 3: "It's not you, it's me."

What gives? he thought. *A few years ago, girls were literally throwing themselves at me after that silly "Christian Bachelor" prank. Now I can't even get* one *date.*

Andy invited Mitch out for wings to pick his brain on how to get to the ladies.

Mitch waited for thirty minutes before a breathless, sweaty Andy slumped into the seat across him. "Sorry, dude. I was working out and lost track of time," he said apologetically. Andy pulled off his hat and revealed a mane of unruly hair. Mitch beheld the forest of curls and wondered if little woodsy creatures would be poking out and joining them for dinner.

"You might want to put your hat back on, man." Mitch said. "It looks like something is living in your hair."

"It's rude to wear a hat inside." Andy countered.

"Right now it's rude not to! And what is that smell? Mitch asked while fanning the air.

"Sorry, man. I ran out of deodorant this morning," Andy said sheepishly.

Mitch scooted his chair back and waived the waitress over. As the evening went on, Andy vented his frustration regarding the numerous rejections he was receiving.

"I don't understand why I can't get dates anymore," Andy complained as he scarfed down his plate of wings.

"You want a napkin, dude?" Mitch asked as he watched the sauce run down Andy's arms to his elbows.

"No, thanks, man," Andy replied and wiped his hands on his shorts. "I mean, I had to fight the girls off a few years ago. Why the sudden cold shoulder?"

"I think you were a little more put together back then," Mitch offered.

"What's wrong with how I am put together now?" Andy asked while unsuccessfully stifling a loud belch.

"Are you serious, man?" Mitch asked. "Look at yourself!"

Andy looked over at his reflection in the restaurant window and self-consciously smoothed his hair back.

"I'll admit I have gotten a little rough around the edges, but this is who I am," Andy argued. "I don't want to present a fake version of myself."

"I am not suggesting that you present a *fake* version of yourself," Mitch assured him. "I am suggesting that you present the *best* version of yourself."

Andy blinked silently in wonder as a light bulb popped on in his head. The next time Mitch saw him, he arrived on time, dressed in a clean new shirt, with a fresh haircut, and smelled like Axe aftershave.

Mitch slapped him on the back. "There's the chick magnet we all know and love! You'll be fighting off the ladies again in no time."

Andy remembered a girl from his past, Anne, whom he had met at that SOS Club coffee shop get-together some time ago. He called her up and asked if she would like to have coffee there again. When she arrived, she accidentally walked right past his table. He looked so different that she didn't even recognize him. The thick Coke bottle glasses were gone, replaced with sleek frames highlighting his beautiful eyes. His formerly shaggy beard was now nicely trimmed to accentuate his chiseled facial features. She had always thought of Andy as a friend, but now, for the first time, looking at him gave her butterflies. Maybe they could be something more.

Peacocking

Although most pictures of peacocks show them with their fantastic feathers fanned out, that is not their modus operandi. Usually, they are just goofy-looking birds dragging around a huge pile of feathers. However, when the female peacocks come around, the males intentionally fan their famed tail feathers and become immediate show-stoppers. Peacocks get it. Bird brain or not, they understand the importance of physical appearance when attracting a mate.

Ladies and gentlemen, the idea that looks don't matter is a lie. Sorry. Looks don't matter as much as inner character, but they *do* matter. Often they determine whether or not your inner character gets a chance to shine.

During my third year of college, I too experienced a significant dating dry spell. I was overwhelmed with school/work and just ready to be done. I rarely took time to put on makeup or even fix my hair. I also did not have many nice clothes. I was on a college student's budget and too proud to ask my parents for help. On top of that, because of stress and harsh facial cleansers, my face was broken out constantly. I was a perfect candidate for Stacy and Clinton on the TV show *What Not to Wear.*

I was rather clueless concerning my unkempt appearance and never considered that it might be contributing to my unwanted singleness. Then as I complained about my solo status one day, a friend decided to get honest with me.

"Harmony, you're one of the prettiest girls I know, but your beauty is hidden because you don't put any effort into your appearance. If you want guys to notice you, start taking better care of yourself and dressing nicer."

Gotta love those honest friends. Unfortunately, I didn't listen to her right away. Fast forward to the year I graduated, I was interviewing for all sorts of design jobs and not getting any callbacks. Enter the honest friend again.

"Harmony, you're not dressing right." *Here we go again.* "You're trying to get a job as a design expert. You have to show people you have a little flavor. You need to look like you stepped out of a magazine. If you look fabulous, you are going to act fabulous."

This time I listened. Extreme makeover, here I come. I went down to the mall, credit card in hand, and did exactly as she said. I put together the snazziest outfit I could. Do you know what happened? I wore my new "power outfit" on my next interview and got the job!

What about you? Do you need an extreme makeover moment? Let's do a little personal evaluation and find out.

Personal Evaluation Checklist

Hair

Has it been cut and styled recently? If not, take some time to freshen up your look. If you're unsure what style is best for you, then book an appointment at a salon and consult a stylist.

Face

Are you taking good care of your skin? Are you using the right cleanser and moisturizer for your skin type to avoid breakouts? If you don't know, consult a dermatologist. Once I finally learned how to properly care for my skin, my decade of struggle with acne ended.

Makeup

If you wear makeup, take some time to brush up on your application skills. Sephora offers complimentary makeup consultations. Learning how to wield this tool to highlight and accentuate your best features can be invaluable.

Facial Hair

Gentlemen, please pick a look and maintain it.

- Clean-shaven? Keep it clean.

- Five-o'clock shadow? Buzz it daily. Shaggy six o'clock comes swiftly.
- Beard? Trim it to follow the lines of your face.
- Duck dynasty foot long? I got no tips on that. Personally, I would feel like I was kissing a broom, but to each their own.

Clothes

Fit: Make sure you are wearing clothes that are the right size. Avoid overly tight or loose.

Style: Are your clothes currently in fashion? If you're unsure, just go to the mall and look at what the mannequins are wearing. I'm serious! The stores have done their homework on what is currently in fashion.

This list is in no way exhaustive, but it will get you started. Use the goods God gave you to their full potential. Make adjustments to better yourself. Simple changes can lead to life-changing results.

Heal Your Wounds

In addition to presenting the best version of yourself physically, you will also want to be sure you are offering the best version of yourself emotionally. Life is hard, and sometimes we are single for a prolonged period because we have emotional wounds preventing us from having healthy relationships.

After my breakup with Ricky, I could not bring myself to date again. I knew I had some emotional wounds I needed to address, but I didn't know where to begin.

My church had a ministry that offered counseling from trained biblical counselors that I was encouraged to try. It took me several weeks to find the courage to even call and inquire about it. The first step was to fill out a back story on myself to match me with a counselor. The back story made me realize that my struggles went further back than the breakup. The counseling office matched me with a counselor and set up an appointment.

I walked into the first counseling session filled with anxiety. How could I possibly face all the pain inside of me? What if the counselor judged me?

"Hi there, Harmony!" said a soft, kind voice.

An elderly man was walking toward me, and before I knew what was happening, he wrapped me in a grandfatherly hug. Then he invited me to join him and the lady, who was his partner, in his counseling office.

"Tell me your story, Harmony," he invited me in a reassuring tone.

With that, the flood gates were opened. A sea of pain came flowing out of me. I talked and cried for over an hour. He never flinched. He just listened empathetically and occasionally offered words of comfort or advice.

The first few sessions were brutal. Digging up the pain was very difficult. At first, I wondered if the sessions were even helping. I didn't realize it at the time, but the pain I was experiencing was a sign that the emotional infection was draining. Eventually, the tears stopped, and the pain dried up. I cried less and then not at all. I began to look forward to my weekly talks with "Grandpa." God used him mightily in my life to guide me to freedom from emotional wounds that were keeping me stuck in singleness.

Mental health is crucial to our well-being and the success of our relationships. Life is hard, and having a safe place to process things with the help of a trained therapist is invaluable. Do not neglect your mental health if professional counseling is not an option for you. When I first began attending counseling, I was on a student's budget and had no insurance. Trust me, where there is a will, there is a way.

I recommend contacting local churches and seeing if they

have a counseling ministry. Also, you can contact local seminaries or graduate schools with counseling programs. Some offer free counseling services to the community so that the students can earn their hours toward certification. Also, some counseling centers offer income-based rates to prevent barriers to entry.

Please do not neglect your mental health because you think your issues are not big enough to warrant help. Regular counseling can help you deal with mild issues before they become big problems. Think about it like this: If you get a pebble in your shoe and take care of it quickly, it will only mildly irritate you. However, if you ignore that pebble because it's no big deal, it will eventually cut into your foot. If you don't take care of the cut, it will become infected. An untreated infection can lead to an amputated foot. So much trouble can come from one little pebble. Take care of your pebble issues now, so they don't have a chance to become crippling.

Last, do not neglect your mental health because you are embarrassed to seek counseling. Our mental and emotional health requires attention and effort, just like our physical health. Some of the healthiest people I know are the ones who frequent their therapist's office. Take care of yourself physically, mentally, and emotionally. You are worth it.

Social Skills

The last personal aspect you need to be mindful of is how you present yourself socially. You may have your appearance and emotional side in tip-top shape, but you may still get friend-zoned if you lack social graces.

While navigating the various dating pools, I had another one of those happenstance meet-cutes. One night, at a singles gathering, a hunky Brad Pitt look-alike showed up. I was immediately attracted to him. We flirted back and forth for a few weeks. Finally, one night the singles group went out to eat together after the service, and my crush came over and sat next to me. I was so happy to finally have the opportunity to have a real conversation with him. Things were going great until one of the other guys asked him for bodybuilding tips. I believe his exact words were, "Eat more protein. I ate so much protein in college that I didn't have a solid BM for two years."

Actually, his exact words were too crud to print, but you get the idea. It was over for me after that. Try as I might, I could never look at him again without thinking of bathroom business. Needless to say, dating him was entirely off the table after that.

Hear me, gentlemen! No woman wants to hear about your bowel movements—*ever.* Save the bathroom humor for the boys. If you need some coaching, find a mom, a sister, an aunt, or someone you can take on a practice date to learn how to talk to a lady. Please!

Same goes for the ladies. A male friend shared with me that he had a crush on a beautiful girl in his music class while in college. He was having a hard time working up the nerve to talk to her, so he wrote her a poem instead. It must have been good because he got a date out of it. Sadly, the evening didn't go well.

"She was really pretty until she opened her mouth," he recalled. "She spent the entire date talking about nothing but herself. Every topic was egocentric and shallow."

Ladies, I know I just spent an entire section talking about peacocking, but beauty without substance is a waste. Just like the proverb says, "A beautiful woman who rejects good sense is like a gold ring in a pig's snout" (*Proverbs 11:22*).

Good sense not only refers to book-smarts but also people-smarts. People-smarts is sometimes referred to as emotional intelligence. One aspect of emotional intelligence is social skills. Poor social skills are another culprit that could be hindering your love life. The trouble with identifying whether or not your social skills need improvement is that it takes social skills to realize that they need improvement.

Here is another time when honest friends can come in handy. If you have been putting off your love interests, ask a trusted friend if you are doing or saying something that might be coming off wrong. You can also be intentional about observing others' reactions to you. Notice what things people respond favorably to and what makes them uncomfortable. Here is a helpful list of some top social skills to be aware of:

Empathy

Prioritize others' needs and feelings. For example, notice if someone appears uncomfortable or at ease, happy or upset, then respond accordingly.

Are you at an outdoor event and notice that your date is shivering? Offer them your jacket, or get them a hot drink.

Are you working the room at a party and your date is holding back and keeping to themselves? Suggest a one-on-one activity with them, or take them somewhere else.

Be mindful of others. Communicating that you care about them doesn't take a lot of effort and pays huge dividends in terms of being liked and trusted.

Nonverbal Communication

Studies show that a large percentage of communication is done through nonverbal cues. Pay attention to others' body language, facial expressions, and tone of voice. This will tell you way more than their words.

Is the person you are talking to smiling, leaning in, and eagerly listening? They are probably enjoying the conversation.

Are they turned away from you, looking around, and

rarely making eye contact? Then they would probably like the conversation to end.

Be aware of your own nonverbal communication as well. You may be saying all the right things, but if your tone or facial expression doesn't match your words, you will come across as insincere.

Verbal Communication

Learn to clearly and pleasantly express yourself to let others know what you are feeling/need.

- Are you hungry? Say so before you turn into a hangry bear.
- Are you tired and need to go home? Say so before dozing off in the middle of a meaningful conversation.

It would be nice if the other person would just pick up on your nonverbal clues without you having to spell them out, but they might not be as far along in their social journey as you. Communicate plainly and frequently.

Listening

Listening is more than just allowing the other person to speak. Authentic listening means giving the speaker your full attention and taking a genuine interest in what they are saying.

When your date is talking, don't look down at your phone and send a text, not even a quick one. In fact, don't look at your phone at all during a date. Put it on silent. The world can live without you for a few hours.

When they are done talking, don't eagerly move on to whatever you want to talk about. Instead, take time to comment on what they have said to show them that you were paying attention and that you care about what they said.

Pacing

Learn to adjust your pace to better interact with others.

Are you texting your potential love interest twenty times a day and getting short one-word responses ... if any? Take it down a notch, or they might feel smothered.

Is your sweetheart always texting sweet messages and your responses are brief and sent hours later ... if at all? Pick up the pace, or you might lose them.

To fully address the topic of social skills and emotional intelligence is beyond the scope of this chapter. If you want more help, I recommend looking into books specializing in these topics. But for now, the skills I mentioned should be enough to get you started on the road to being your best self.

CHAPTER FIFTEEN

The Flat Tire

I was driving through Downtown Dallas, admiring the sunset over the skyline when I heard it.

POP! Thud, thud, thud, thud.

Baby Blue was wounded! One of her tires had been punctured, and I went from rolling to hobbling in seconds.

No! I was on an out-of-town business trip and due to have dinner in an hour with my colleagues. I desperately did not want to miss that and prayed there would be a repair shop nearby to get me road-worthy again. There wasn't. It was less than a mile to my hotel. There was no safe place to pull over, so I was forced to limp alongside traffic. At the same time, the other drivers proceeded to roll down their windows to offer helpful comments.

"Ma'am! You have a flat tire!"

Thank you, Captain Obvious! I'd stop right here and change it in the middle of this busy street, but somehow that seems counterproductive.

We continued our trek of shame 'til we reached the safety of the hotel parking garage. I called for a tow, but they said their tow truck could not fit inside the garage. Instead, they recommended I find the nearest tire and lube shop and limp my way there. So

I did. Again, it was less than a mile away. I put the address into my GPS and hobbled onward. Unfortunately, I overlooked just one tiny detail about my tidy little Google map route—it was via the freeway.

I realized too late that I had been directed into multiple lanes of cars going 70+ mph. Still, poor Baby Blue was barely capable of 20 mph in her condition. The freeway drivers had absolutely no pity on either of us. We were honked at and whizzed past mercilessly as I frantically hugged the shoulder and prayed for a nearby exit. I eventually found one, only to find myself in the absolute ghetto of Dallas, so much so that a policewoman came to sit with me while I waited until 9:00 p.m. for the Fix-a-Flat guy to show up.

Needless to say, I didn't make it to dinner that night. My trip home the following day was delayed after visiting the tire shop, and I was several hundred dollars poorer.

After all that trouble, I thought my flat tire was toast, but it just needed to have the puncture sealed and the correct amount of air pumped back into it. Tires are all about boundaries. They only function correctly when the air within the tire remains at the proper pounds per square inch (PSI). Any breach in the rubber boundary will immediately begin to deflate the tire; it might happen slowly and subtly or go out with a bang as it did in my case. Still, one way or the other, tires without boundaries will get you nowhere.

On the road to marriage, you will find that your response to one of God's boundaries may determine whether you roll or thud to the altar. It's time, my friends, for the sex talk …

And God Said Have Sex!

If you are like me, most of what you have heard on the biblical stance concerning sex can be summed up in one word—NO!

To be fair, the Bible does have quite a lot to say against sexual immorality.

> Flee sexual immorality! Every other sin a person commits is outside the body, but the person who is sexually immoral sins against his own body (*1 Corinthians 6:18*).

> Therefore, put to death what belongs to your earthly nature: sexual immorality, impurity, lust, evil desire, and greed, which is idolatry (*Colossians 3:5*).

> For this is God's will, your sanctification: that you keep away from sexual immorality, that each of you knows how to control his own body in holiness and honor (*1 Thessalonians 4:3–4*).

In these verses, sexual immorality is translated from the Greek word *porneia*. Its meanings include fornication (consensual sexual activity between two unmarried people), prostitution, and promiscuity.[36] Basically, sexual immorality is any sexual activity outside of marriage. God does say no to sex a lot. However, there's another side of the story. Before God ever said don't, He said do.

> God blessed them, and God said to them, "Be fruitful, multiply, fill the earth ..." (*Genesis 1:28*)

Right there, in the first chapter, the first words recorded between God and mankind was to go *get it on*. I wasn't there, of course, but I imagine Adam and Eve's response was something like this: "Yeeees, Loooord!"

---

[36] https://biblehub.com/greek/4202.htm

God is not anti-sex. Not only did He command it, but He also provided a how-to manual in Song of Solomon. There's a reason no one ever asks you to read that book aloud in Sunday school!

If God is pro-sex, why is it that the primary biblical stance we hear from the pulpit is a bunch of thou-shalt-not? It's because God designed the sexual relationship to function best within a boundary.

The Boundary

The boundary of marriage is to sex what the rubber boundary is to the tire. The boundary of marriage harnesses sex's power and benefits. Scripture is full of warnings against sexual immorality because, biblically, sex and marriage are inseparable. To understand why, we must go back to the beginning, to the first marriage.

Quick recap—Adam is lonely, so God puts him to sleep, takes one of his ribs, and makes him a companion. Adam joyfully proclaims, "This one, at last, is bone of my bone and flesh of my flesh. This one will be called 'woman' for she was taken from man" (*Genesis 2:23*).

Then the narrator cuts in, "This is why a man leaves his father and mother and bonds with his wife, and they become one flesh" (*Genesis 2:24*).

This is the first mention of marriage in scripture. The family of origin is left to be united with a life partner in a relationship designed to be so intimate that the two become one. God placed sex within the boundaries of marriage because He meant for sex and love to be inseparable. In its purest form, marriage is the most profound expression of love. Think about the vows and their implications.

Marriage is saying, "I choose you and only you, no matter what. I choose to love you when you're sick, be faithful to you when you're distant, be there for you when you're sad, and pick you up when you fall. I choose you to laugh with, cry with, build a life with, and create a family with. You're my person for life."

God designed sex to function within that kind of loving environment. When sex and marriage are separated in a culture, a subtle leak begins, so tiny that it's barely noticeable until an entire society's love life has a blowout.

The Slippery Slope

A culture's values are often communicated through the art that the culture produces. Popular songs, movies, sitcoms, magazines, ads, and the like give us a window into what a culture values and promotes. Let's take a walk down memory lane and look at some cultural output regarding sex, love, and marriage from the last three decades.

Friends (1994 TV sitcom)

A popular sitcom that follows a group of lovable single friends as they navigate life together. The pilot episode introduces us to Rachel frantically fleeing her wedding in favor of clinging to singleness. Her future lover, Ross, has just discovered his wife is leaving him for another woman. His bachelor friends, Chandler and Joey, welcome him back to the club and encourage him to begin enjoying the "good life" again. This attitude that values singleness and avoids marriage continues throughout the series. The underlying message is that the good life is maintaining the freedom of singleness while still enjoying the benefits of sex. Bottom line: Marriage and sex needn't go hand in hand anymore.

Bones (2005 TV show)

In the majorly popular TV series *Bones*—which I love, by the way—all the couples who eventually decide to be monogamous move in together and live happy lives with one foot in singleness and the other in a pseudo marriage for years. When one partner becomes weary of that lifestyle and begins to "push" the other to marry, they are met with resistance from their partner.

"Isn't our shared love enough?"

"Why do we need a piece of paper to validate our commitment to each other?"

"If you really loved me, you wouldn't pressure me."

The party seeking marriage eventually repents and declares that their love is enough. Loving someone is defined as willingly sharing life, home, bed, and children with them without requiring marriage commitment.

First, marriage and sex were separated; now marriage and love have also been parted.

No Strings Attached (2011 movie)

In this hit movie, Emma and Adam are lifelong friends who decide they want each other's bodies but not each other's hearts. Love is a messy business that neither wants to deal with. So they make a pact to make their relationship strictly physical and avoid falling in love at all costs. The plot follows their struggle to engage in sex without developing romantic feelings. Eventually, the characters fall in love despite their original intentions to just use each other sexually.

Once the culture liberated itself from marriage, it became popular to throw off the troubles of love as well. Friends with benefits became acceptable as long as it was consensual. So now sex is not only separated from marriage but also from love.

"Shape of You" (2017 pop song)

Ed Sheeran's hit single broke records the year it was released. The beat is excellent, so much so that it is now stuck in my head. However, the message of the song is horrible. The song tells the story of strangers who meet at a bar. They skip the small talk and get straight to the point—"put that body on me." They go from the bar to the bedroom in one verse, and now the man is in love, not with a person, but with a body.

I'm in love with the shape of you
We push and pull like a magnet do
Although my heart is falling too
I'm in love with your body.

Sex is not only separated from marriage and love but also from the partners themselves. The partners dehumanize each other and themselves by engaging primarily with each other's bodies.

The Fall Out

Art is not only a reflection of culture; it is also an influencer of culture. The art feeds the culture, and the culture feeds the art until the message eventually becomes that culture's worldview. I'll never forget the day I casually mentioned the concept of sexual abstinence until marriage to a friend. Her response shocked me.

"I would never buy a car without test driving it. Why would I marry someone without trying them out first?"

Excuse me?! When did people become objects to be tried out instead of individuals to be loved and respected?

The slippery slope was subtle, but it was there. Did you notice it? First, sex was separated from marriage. Next, marriage was separated from love. Then love was separated from sex. Finally, sex was separated from the souls of the participants. The partners became bodies instead of people. A worldview that cheapens sex also cheapens love, marriage, and people. This leaves many floundering in singleness, looking for love in a context where it cannot be found.

Sex Makes Babies

Another reason God binds sex to marriage is because of the power that sex possesses. Sex creates new life. The first time sex is ever mentioned in the Bible, it is in the context of procreation. If you recall, God's mandate in Genesis 1:28 was to have sex to be fruitful and multiply.

Sex and marriage are to be inseparable because sex and children are inseparable. Have you noticed that all methods of contraception have a little disclaimer? None are guaranteed to work 100 percent of the time. At best, they are 99.99 percent effective. Many of us are living proof that 0.01 percent is all it takes. Sex has the irrefutable power to create new life, and such power is best wielded within a loving, committed marriage.

The final reason for reserving sex for marriage is that God designed our sex drive as a built-in motivator to spur couples to commit to each other and start families. One reason that marriage is postponed or even avoided more than it used to be is the widespread removal of the God-given motivation of sexual frustration. God's solution to sexual frustration outside of marriage is not merely to abstain—it's to get married!

Restore the Boundary

Removing the God-given boundary regarding sex creates a slow leak that can eventually lead to a relational blowout and inadvertently prolong one's season of singleness. When sex is cheap, love and marriage become optional, burdensome even. However, when sex is sacred, love and marriage become privileges worth sacrificing for. If sex outside of marriage has given your love life a flat tire, don't despair. Instead, restore godly boundaries and pump it back up. We've still got a little way to go.

CHAPTER SIXTEEN

Fear

It's the middle of the night. Jesus's disciples are fighting an unexpected storm as they attempt to cross the Sea of Galilee.

"Sure wish Jesus was here," John said in a quivering voice. "We could definitely use His calming-the-wind-and-waves routine about now, but *nooo*, He just *had* to have some alone time."

James rolled his eyes at his kid brother. "Stop being so clingy, John. *You're* probably the reason He wanted alone time. I'm just wondering how He is planning on crossing the lake with no boat."

"I asked Him that, and He muttered something about it being just a short walk," Peter chimed in. "Doesn't He know it would take Him days to walk around this lake?"

"Guys!" John gasped. "Someone is walking on the water!"

"Not now, John," James said exasperated. "We don't have time for your nonsense. Just keep bailing water."

"HE'S HEADING STRAIGHT FOR US!" John shrieked like a little girl.

"John, for the last ti—" James's voice choked off.

A ghostly figure was indeed walking toward the boat. Terrified screams and prayers for deliverance went up as the fear factor on the boat went through the roof. Then a familiar commanding voice broke through the chaos.

"It is I. Don't be afraid" (*Matthew 14:27*).

"Wait … is that … Jesus?"

"Don't be afraid," He says.

He's only taking an eerie midnight stroll across the sea. Nothing creepy to see here. Jesus could've just boarded the boat earlier, but what kind of entrance would that have been?

Peter, as usual, takes charge of the situation. "Lord, if it's you, command me to come to you on the water" (*Matthew 14:28*).

"Come!" (*Matthew 14:29*)

Oh no! The Lord called his bluff. Peter talked big, but did he have the guts to step out? For once, his infamous impetuousness came in handy. He just did it. He stepped out of the boat in the middle of a storm and began walking on the water. This is such a familiar story that we often overlook the fact that *Peter is walking on water*! Talk about a confidence booster. Imagine the next time the other disciples wanted to brag about something.

"Hey, Pete, watch this."

"Whatever, dude, I walked on water."

Sadly, the confidence was short-lived. Once Peter came down from the adrenaline rush, he became very aware of the danger.

> But when he saw the strength of the wind, he was afraid, and beginning to sink he cried out, "Lord, save me!" (*Matthew 14:30*)

The general belief is that Peter sank because he became afraid. I disagree. Peter's mistake was not that he was afraid. It was that he let the fear immobilize him. I don't know much about the physics of walking on water. The closest thing I can compare it to is water skiing. Have you ever gone water skiing? What happens when you stop moving? You sink. Fear thwarted Peter's miracle, and it will thwart your love life too, if you let it.

Catch Her If You Can

Chance is a great catch. He's a successful businessman, a wonderful man of God, and has a great personality. Seriously, if joy and fun were people and they had a baby, it would be him. Misty hates to see a good man go to waste, so she tried to set Chance up with an interested young lady. He was flattered and thought she was gorgeous but decided to pass on the opportunity. Why? Well … he's still getting his footing in his career … His schedule is wonky … He's trying to transfer and doesn't have a home base yet … Excuses, excuses …

"Yeah … I think you're smoke-screening. What's the real reason?" Misty pressed.

"I actually have an old crush I've been working up the nerve to ask out," he admitted.

"Fantastic! When do you plan to let her know you're interested?" she asked with great enthusiasm.

"Well, I'm not sure. I've had a crush on her for forever, but I'm not sure if she's interested, and I would hate to mess up our friendship."

"So … your feelings for someone you don't even think is interested are hindering you from pursuing someone who clearly is interested?" Misty asked again.

"I guess I'm holding out in hopes that she will give me a positive sign or something," he admitted again.

"I see, and how long have you been holding out on this girl?" she asked.

"Several years," he confessed sheepishly.

"What?" Misty exclaimed in disbelief. "Rip the Band-Aid off, dude! Just ask her!"

Why won't Chance take a chance? Simple, he's afraid. Fear can sink your love boat quicker than almost any other human emotion. It will take the wind out of your sails and cause your romantic dreams to grind to an indefinite halt, if you let it.

To be clear, I am not referring to the natural fear that triggers our survival instincts in the presence of an actual threat. I am referring instead to a fear that assumes and prepares for a worst-case scenario without due cause. Fear can be tricky to spot. It is not something people want to readily admit to, so it gets disguised with excuses. Here are a few common examples:

- It's not the right time to be in a relationship.
- God wants me to focus on just Him for now.
- I am waiting 'til I finish school, get the right job, ... and so on.

Have you said things like this to yourself? Do you want to know if any of these reasons are legit or if they are a smoke screen for fear? Here's a quick test: Suppose the person of your dreams offered you a relationship tomorrow, and you knew it would work out. Would you reject it because you needed to focus on God, school, or work? If the answer is yes, then go ahead and skip this chapter. However, if you are already blissfully imagining yourself halfway to the altar with your dream spouse, then may I suggest that your true motivation for not pursuing a relationship is fear?

> For God has not given us a spirit of fear, but one of power, love, and sound judgment (*2 Timothy 1:7*).

There is a spirit of fear, but it is not of God. The spirit of fear is a liar. He twists the natural instinct of fear to create feelings of dread and anxiety when no actual threat is present.

The spirit of fear tells you that you will fail relationally, so don't even try. It tells you that the reward of love is not worth the risk of rejection. It tells you it is better to stay in the boat of your status quo instead of following God out onto the water. If you let it, fear will enslave you and keep you stuck in singleness. Let's look at the most common fears that hinder relationships.

Rejection

"What if they aren't interested in me and turn me down?"

If you want, you could try to do a little subtle recon to gauge their level of interest. Do you have any mutual friends who could be trusted to casually suggest to your person of interest the possibility of dating you? Their reaction will tell you everything. I know it's a bit middle school, but hey, so is dating. If you don't want to go that route, then take a risk and let the chips fall where they may. It's better to risk rejection now than put off pursuing them until "the right time." This will lead you to develop an attachment to them based on a future relationship that only exists in your imagination. Having your dreams dashed after spending months working up the courage to ask is way worse. Just rip the Band-Aid off. If they say "No, thanks," that's OK. Rejection hurts, but it is a part of life. Reframe rejection as redirection. Your affections are being redirected elsewhere.

Loss

"What if asking them out ruins our friendship?"

If your friendship is so fragile that it will be ruined by you expressing that you admire them enough to want to know them on a deeper level, then let it go. It will be awkward for a while if they turn you down. Push through the awkwardness and get on with life. However, you may find that later they change their mind and revisit the topic with you. I have a happily married friend who needed to see her current husband move past his interest in her to realize she had feelings for him.

Failure

"What if it doesn't work out and we have to break up?"

That's okay. Every dating relationship will eventually end. It will either end in a breakup or a marriage. Acknowledge that fact and proceed accordingly. Treat each other with kindness and respect to minimize (notice I didn't say eliminate) regret. To err is human.

"What if we get married and it ends in divorce?"

I can't promise you that won't happen. The prevalence of divorce is an excellent reason to feel reluctant to enter marriage. But is avoiding the possibility of divorce worth denying yourself the experience of marriage? Only you can decide that.

My dad is an avid swimmer who doesn't like pools. He prefers to swim in the great outdoors. He lives in Florida, so he has ample options of the ocean, rivers, lakes, springs, and large creeks. His swimming holes are beautiful, but some are also alligator alley.

"Are you ever afraid that one of those gators might decide to take a bite out of you?" I asked him once.

"Yes, but my desire to swim is greater than my fear of the gators," he said like a true Cajun.

So which is greater, your fear of failure or your desire for love?

Heartbreak

"What if I get my heart broken?"

Experiencing grief is a part of life. The only way to avoid relational pain is to avoid relationships. All people will hurt you at times, especially the one you eventually choose to marry. Imagine two sinful humans in a lifelong permanent relationship—that is a recipe for heartbreak. If you don't want any chance of getting your heart broken, put this book down and choose the gift of singleness.

The spirit of fear will influence you to imagine a dozen more negative outcomes, but what if we silence it for a moment and imagine positive alternatives instead?

- What if they are also interested in you and will be elated when you ask them out?

- What if you enhance your friendship by becoming a couple and end up dating your best friend?
- What if it does work out and you find that you are a great fit?
- What if your heart falls deeply in love?

These positive scenarios are just as likely, if not more so, than their negative alternatives. However, to make them realities, you will have to silence the spirit of fear.

Neutralize Fear

Overcoming fear is not as simple as just deciding not to be afraid. We have to use the tools given to us to defeat fear. The Bible gives us three arrows to fire when the spirit of fear rears its ugly head.

> For God has not given us a spirit of fear, but one of *power*, *love*, and *sound judgment* (*2 Timothy 1:7*).

Power

Power stands up to fear and says, "You're not in control; God is."

As a believer, you have the power of God himself working within you.

> Now to him who is able to do above and beyond all that we ask or think according to the power that works in us (*Ephesians 3:20*).

> The weapons of our warfare are not of the flesh, but are powerful through God for the demolition of strongholds (*2 Corinthians 10:4*).

God can accomplish more than you could even imagine. Your wildest dreams haven't even come close to what God's power is capable of. Use the powerful spiritual weapons at your disposal to tear down the stronghold of fear holding you captive. One of these weapons is love.

Love

Love neutralizes fear. Love is to fear what light is to darkness. The two cannot coexist.

> There is no fear in love; instead, perfect love drives out fear (*1 John 4:18*).

Once when I took my youth to a summer camp, I spotted a student sitting on the side of the pool looking wistfully at her friends swimming.

"Why aren't you getting in?" I asked.

"I can't swim," she said, head down.

"Sure you can," I assured her. "I'll teach you. Get in."

She dutifully got in but remained glued to the ladder. I stretched out my arms beside her and told her to lay across them. She did, and we proceeded to move across the pool. She was able to concentrate on her swimming strokes, uninhibited by fear, because she could feel my arms beneath her. Once she got the hang of it, I subtly lowered my arms a fraction of an inch. As soon as she couldn't feel me anymore, she gave me a look of panic and immediately started to sink.

"Keep swimming! My hands are still right underneath you," I assured her again.

I made contact briefly and then lowered my arms again. Her look of panic turned to a look of confidence. She swam the distance of that pool unaided because she trusted that I loved her and would catch her if she faltered. That's how love casts out fear. Just as my arms guarded her, God's arms guard you.

The God of old is your dwelling place, and underneath are the everlasting arms. He drives out the enemy before you and commands, "Destroy!" (*Deuteronomy 33:27*)

For I am persuaded that neither death nor life, nor angels nor rulers, nor things present nor things to come, nor powers, nor height nor depth, nor any other created thing will be able to separate us from the love of God that is in Christ Jesus our Lord (*Romans 8:38–39*).

There is absolutely nothing that can separate you from the love of God. What's more, God Himself has your back, and because of this, there is nothing in heaven or earth that can successfully stand against you.

If God is for us, who can be against us? (*Romans 8:31 NIV*)

This is the kind of love that neutralizes fear. Let it give you the confidence to step out and do the things you are afraid of.

Sound Judgment

Sound judgment challenges fear. It looks at fear's declarations of doom and says, "It doesn't have to be that way." A godly mind is the key to making sound judgments.

Do not be conformed to this age, but be transformed by the renewing of your mind, so that you may discern what is the good, pleasing, and perfect will of God (*Romans 12:2*).

One way to renew your mind is through a regular intake of God's Word. Have you heard, "You are what you think"? Well, what you think depends on what you ingest mentally. Therefore, a mind filled with God's Word will be guided by God's Spirit.

Sound judgment is the natural output of a mind controlled by the Spirit of God. Sound judgment will enable you to discern God's will. With this discernment comes wisdom. Wisdom and discernment give us the ability to make wise decisions that typically result in success instead of failure. They protect us by revealing what is good, right, and godly so that we can avoid what is not. Finally, sound judgment enables us to act with confidence. Confidence is crucial to defeating fear. Ironically, confidence comes from facing and overcoming your fears.

Remember good old Chance? He finally worked up the courage to ask his longtime crush out. Guess what happened—he got flat-out rejected, and he was so glad.

"I'm so glad I asked because her rejection gave me confidence," he shared. "My worst fear came true, and it wasn't that bad. I didn't die. It actually made me less scared of rejection and more likely to take a chance in the future."

Take a chance he did. Once his heart was no longer tethered to his old crush, he was able to notice the favorable attention of a lovely girl right in front of him. He asked her out promptly and married her a year later.

Ironically, facing his fear head on—and even experiencing it—gave Chance the confidence to pursue the woman who eventually became his wife.

To feel fear does not mean that you're a coward. On the contrary, boldness is taking action in the presence of fear. Do you want to do what it takes to move out of singleness but you still feel afraid? That's OK. Do it anyway. Don't wait until you are free of fear to act. That will never happen. Put on your Nikes and *just do it*. You might fail, and that's OK. Permission to fail is permission to live. The more you face your fears, the less scary they will be.

Even if you start strong and end up wigging out halfway through, that's OK. Notice Jesus's reaction when Peter began to sink because of fear.

> Immediately Jesus reached out his hand, caught hold of him, and said to him, "You of little faith, why did you doubt?" (*Matthew 14:31*)

Despite his lack of faith, Jesus would not leave Peter high and dry (or low and wet, in this case). Jesus had his back regardless, and He's got yours too. Jesus continually repeated, "Do not be afraid," to assure His disciples and us that He's got this and He's got us. He won't let us down even if our fears do get the better of us.

Have you ever wondered what would have happened if Peter had pushed past his fear and kept walking? Would his courage have inspired the rest of the disciples to step out too? Would they all have just walked to the shore and invited the waiting crowd to join them? Sadly, we'll never know. However, you can still find out what will happen if you trust God and push through your fears.

- Are you afraid of rejection? Pursue anyway.
- Are you afraid of failing? Try anyway.
- Are you afraid of heartbreak? Love anyway.
- Are you afraid of permanent singleness? Date anyway.

If you *do it anyway* often enough, one day, when fear taunts, "You can't do it," you will reply, "Oh really? I just did."

CHAPTER SEVENTEEN

Dare to Hope

The chapel was filled with smiling faces that morning, except for mine. My face reflected the hopelessness in my heart. I was coming up on the anniversary of when I first began hoping and praying for a spouse. Approximately a year ago, I started my journey to escape singleness. I tackled unbiblical doctrines, challenged cultural expectations, and overcame personal hindrances. Yet I was still just as single as when I started. A friend who knew my story kindly asked if I was all right. Before I could stop myself, I blurted out, "I'm sick of waiting, sick of trying, and I'm sick of praying!"

Hope is a very powerful thing, but delayed hope is also very powerful. God Himself says that delayed hope makes the heart sick (Proverbs 13:12). Hope for something that is delayed repeatedly and seemingly indefinitely can suck the life out of you. I was weary to the bone. I was heart sick. I was sorry I had ever begun my quest and was ready to give up on the spouse-search altogether. I felt there was no hope left in me.

Although I didn't know it at the time, the suffering I experienced from delayed hope produced the mature hope I needed to see rise out of the ashes of my disappointment. Hope is one of those virtues that must be developed. Hope is like patience. Have you ever prayed for patience? Let me warn you, pray for patience and you will have many annoying reasons to practice patience coming your way. There is a particular path to producing hope, and it begins with suffering.

> ³We also boast in our afflictions, because we know that affliction produces endurance, ⁴endurance produces proven character, and proven character produces hope. ⁵This hope will not disappoint us ... (*Romans 5:3–5*)

Gym buffs understand this principle. Just look at their slogans:

1. No pain, no gain.
2. Pain is weakness leaving the body.
3. The pain you feel today will be the strength you feel tomorrow.

No bodybuilder walks into a gym and purchases chiseled abs and bulging forearms. Instead, they purchase the privilege of using the gym's various torture devices to develop those abs and arms. Hope muscles are the same. The strength necessary to accomplish your dreams comes from the times you struggled. Hope produced from overcoming affliction is a seasoned, mature hope that does not disappoint.

Hope Defined

Mature hope is not just wishful or positive thinking. It combines a can-be belief with a can-do attitude. It doesn't just wish for good things; it takes action to make them happen. It is not daunted when the results are not immediate. Hope dares to look failure and disappointment in the face and declare victory over them. It refuses to resign itself to the status quo and relentlessly pursues the life that could be. It opens the door to possibilities and inspires us to pursue our goals and dreams fervently.

Paul lists hope among the top three Christian virtues. Combined with faith and love, hope is essential to living a fulfilled life. Faith inspires us, love motivates us, but hope empowers us. The power of hope lies in its source.

> But those who hope in the LORD will renew their strength. They will soar on wings like eagles; they will run and not grow weary, they will walk and not be faint (*Isaiah 40:31 NIV*).

> Why, my soul, are you so dejected? Why are you in such turmoil? Put your hope in God, for I will still praise him, my Savior and my God (*Psalm 42:5*).

The source of your hope is the Lord Himself. As a child of God, you have access to the very power that raised Jesus from the dead. The God of all creation gave His life for you and loves you with an everlasting love. When God is for you, no power in heaven or on earth can withstand you.

Hope Restored

Even though my hope muscles were strong, they were tired. God knew I was suffering from hope fatigue that Sunday morning, so He sent me an opportunity for respite. The speaker at church that morning was the head of a thriving missionary organization in India. I listened in wonder as he described the work his team was doing. I had been fascinated with India ever since I was in high school. My hero as a teenager was Amy Carmichael, the Irish missionary who had spent her life in India rescuing children from sexual exploitation. I had longed to follow in her footsteps and make a difference for those who needed it most, but the opportunity had never come until now. The speaker announced that our church was assembling a team to go to minister in India on a short-term mission trip. The moment the words were out of his mouth, I knew God was calling me to go. When the service ended, I practically bolted to the office of the mission's pastor to sign up.

The cost to go just happened to be my life's savings, which I had intentionally set aside to cover the wedding I had been sure was coming. I was advised to send out support letters for financial aid but warned that I would be responsible for any remaining balance. What if no one offered to help me? Was I willing to watch my wedding fund go up in smoke permanently? My desire to go to India far outweighed my desire to protect my net worth. I signed on the dotted line and began preparing for the journey: passport, shots, time off work. Everything was ready, except for the funds.

There were only a few weeks left before we left. My traveling companions had received total funding for the trip weeks ago. I still had over halfway to go. I imagined my savings account balance becoming a big goose egg. I felt God remind me of my commitment to go to India, no matter what, and I let it all go. It was just money; I could always earn more. Do you know what happened? Right before I signed away my savings, an anonymous donor covered all but $200 of the cost at the last minute. I didn't know it at the time, but God was restoring my hope bit by bit by giving me opportunities to see Him work on my behalf in real time.

Going to India was the best experience of my life. While there, I saw a way of living for God that blew my American version of Christianity out of the water. The people I met had a devotion and passion for the Lord that I had never seen before. I taught biblical truth to people who should have been teaching me how to truly live for God.

In addition to the spiritual aspects, I also reveled in the cultural and culinary aspects of the country. The land of India is truly fascinating. Never had I seen such colors, been shown such hospitality, or encountered such desperate poverty. The people I ministered to ate nothing but rice and lentils. Yet they rolled out the red carpet and provided my team and me with such an Indian feast that I almost felt ashamed to eat it. Notice I said *almost.* Indian food is fantastic. I put on ten pounds while we were there.

Out of all the amazing things I experienced, what made the biggest impression on me was the attitude of the Indian people toward life and God. Despite the extreme poverty and dangers associated with practicing Christianity, their attitude was humble gratitude and in awe of the God who saved them. There was no entitlement, no asking God why He had blessed others with such abundance while they suffered such deprivation. Only complete abandon and devotion to the Lord and His calling to spread the Gospel.

I went to India hopeless and dejected, but I left with a fresh perspective and hopeful outlook. I still longed for a husband, but that longing no longer consumed me. I no longer felt like God owed me a spouse. Instead, I was determined to live the Christian life to the fullest like my Indian friends, which meant a life of thankfulness.

Now, why have I spent so much time gushing about India whenever I am supposed to be telling you the path out of singleness? I tell you this story because, despite our best efforts, the path out of singleness can still be long and discouraging. You may also suffer from the effects of delayed hope and want to give up. When you hit that wall, instead of quitting, take a break. Step out of the dating game and focus on something else. Find an avenue to walk with God, where His work is more apparent. Give your hope muscles a rest and work on thankfulness. You will find that a rested hope often leads to a renewed hope.

Hope Renewed

I would be graduating from seminary soon, and it was time to begin planning the next phase of my life. After my great experience in India, I was interested in exploring what opportunities there were to return. I applied with the International Mission Board for a position ministering to women in Nepal and looked into student ministry openings in the States. The world was my oyster, and I couldn't wait to see what God had for me. My heart was light, and my hope was high. It's a good thing because I was about to be taking the biggest faith leap of my life, but it wasn't to Nepal.

I was sitting in my chair, trying to focus on reading a giant theological book.

Ding!

Saved by the text. I didn't recognize the number. Who could this be?

> "Hi, Harmony, it has been a while since we have talked. I am in a better place emotionally, and I would like to know if I could have your permission to call you again this evening."
> —Mr. Match

I broke into a huge smile. The one that got away had come back.

"Hey! I would love to talk again. I'll be free after 8."

We had a great talk that night. As the conversation ended, he politely suggested that we meet in person to see if we "clicked" in real life.

Why not? What have I got to lose?

I agreed, and we made a date for the upcoming week. He had asked if I preferred to have him pick me up or if I wanted to meet somewhere. Meet somewhere definitely. If this guy was a creeper, I didn't want him to know where I lived, and I wanted my getaway car at the ready. A girl can't be too careful. I suggested my favorite restaurant, a hipster burger joint on Magnolia Avenue.

When the day came, I dressed carefully. I wanted to look attractive and slightly alluring but nowhere near loose or provocative. Ultimately, I chose my zebra print cashmere sweater, skinny jeans, tall black leather boots, and my bright red Calvin Klein wool coat. I arrived early and positioned myself on the back patio, where I knew he would have to pass by. I had brought my Bible. I felt it would help my cause as a prospective godly wife to be found reading God's Word as he approached. Yes, I did put that much thought into it, and no, it was not an act. I could be found quite often reading God's Word with no ulterior motives, just not that day. Girls peacock too, you know.

He arrived promptly. I heard footsteps coming up behind me and knew it was him. We greeted each other and exchanged one of those semi-awkward Baptist side hugs. We had a great lunch with good conversation. As the meal drew close, he casually asked if I would like to ride together or separately to the next phase of our date. Wait, what? He had actually planned something else himself? Usually, all the guys just sat back and let me plan everything. I had not been taken on a date I didn't plan in over a year. Intrigued, I decided we could ride together. I felt confident by this point that he was not a creeper.

He took me to the IMAX theatre in Downtown Fort Worth. It was so cool and such a different experience. Luckily, I had not scheduled anything else for that day because when it was over, he said we had one more stop to make. So off to the Fort Worth Water Gardens we went. While there, he pulled out all our exchanges on the dating platform and asked me to further elaborate on my responses. He was so eager to get to know me better. I felt so noticed and cared about.

After a great first date, he brought me back to my car. He looked at me sheepishly and then reached over and patted my hand several times. I wasn't sure how to respond. I certainly wasn't going to awkwardly pat him back. I said goodbye and quickly got out of the car before he started patting my head or something. Despite the awkwardness of his farewell, I decided to give him a second date and a third and a fourth. Mr. Match intrigued me. He was unlike any other man I had ever known. In many ways, he was a walking contradiction. He worked on cars, remodeled houses, and wrote poetry and love songs. He was so intellectual that he was like a walking encyclopedia, but he was also so goofy that he performed skits with his eyebrows, turning them into Hispanic lovers, both vying for my affections; the eyebrows of love, he would call them. He seemed to be the best of all worlds. It was as if the man of my dreams had suddenly taken on human form. Although I was skeptical that he might be too good to be true, I decided to stick around and find out.

Hope Rewarded

You know you're in love when you can't fall asleep because reality is finally better than your dreams.
—Dr. Seuss

"You're Beautiful" by Phil Wickham resonated throughout the chapel as I stood in a glistening wedding gown, waiting for my cue to enter. My season of singleness was coming to a close. Mr. Match had turned out to be a keeper. As the song drifted past the double doors into my ears, my mind drifted back to the countless moments that had brought me here. I recalled the heartbreak that had begun this journey. I realized that there, in my darkest moment, the Lord was weaving a plan that would lead me to this moment of triumph.

My journey out of singleness had been full of many twists and turns that all added up to making my current reality possible. I was living an answered prayer, and it was a beautiful thing. The day had been like a dream, but it wasn't. This was my reality—my wonderful, inspiring, faith-building reality. My story had come full circle because my God specializes in giving beauty for ashes. My time of reflection came to an end as the song reached a crescendo and the chapel doors swung open. My husband and my future were waiting for me. It was time to walk into the next chapter of my story.

This, my friends, is what is possible when you dare to hope. My once empty arms now hold a husband and three sons because "nothing will be impossible with God" (*Luke 1:37*).

Now it's your turn. Will you choose to hope by actively participating in the life God has given you? Your season of singleness need only be a section in your book. It's not the whole story. The Lord sees where you are, but He also sees where you will be. Dare to see your future as the Lord does. Dare to hope.

Made in the USA
Las Vegas, NV
30 July 2023